PLACES
PUBLIC ARCHITECTURE

HCMA ARCHITECTURE+DESIGN

Edited by Alexandra Kenyon
Foreword by Christopher Macdonald
With contributions by Darryl Condon, Jim Taggart, and Melissa Higgs

ORO Editions
Publishers of Architecture, Art, and Design
Gordon Goff: Publisher

www.oroeditions.com
info@oroeditions.com

Published by ORO Editions

Copyright © ORO Editions, 2015
Text and Images © HCMA Architecture+Design, 2015

All rights reserved. No part of this book may be reproduced, stored in a retrieval system, or transmitted in any form or by any means, including electronic, mechanical, photocopying of microfilming, recording, or otherwise (except that copying permitted by Sections 107 and 108 of the U.S. Copyright Law and except by reviewers for the public press) without written permission from the publisher.

You must not circulate this book in any other binding or cover and you must impose this same condition on any acquirer.

Book Design: Pablo Mandel
This book has been typeset in Akzidenz-Grotesk

Edited by Alexandra Kenyon
Texts by Christopher Macdonald, Darryl Condon, Jim Taggart and Melissa Higgs

10 9 8 7 6 5 4 3 2 1 First Edition

Library of Congress data available upon request. World Rights: Available

ISBN: 978-1-941806-44-9

Color Separations and Printing: ORO Group Ltd.
Printed in Hong Kong.

International Distribution: www.oroeditions.com/distribution

ORO Editions makes a continuous effort to minimize the overall carbon footprint of its publications. As part of this goal, ORO Editions, in association with Global ReLeaf, arranges to plant trees to replace those used in the manufacturing of the paper produced for its books. Global ReLeaf is an international campaign run by American Forests, one of the world's oldest nonprofit conservation organizations. Global ReLeaf is American Forests' education and action program that helps individuals, organizations, agencies, and corporations improve the local and global environment by planting and caring for trees.

Contents

8	**Foreword**	by Christopher Macdonald
10	**Places Manifesto**	by Darryl Condon
12	**Toward Social Sustainability**	by Jim Taggart
20	**From Temples of the Mind to the People's Temple**	by Darryl Condon

28	**Whistler Library**	WHISTLER BC
46	**Duchess Park Secondary**	PRINCE GEORGE BC
64	**Steveston Firehall**	RICHMOND BC

76	**HCMA Culture**
78	**HCMA Day**
88	**Building Blocks Playhouse**
94	**Wall House**
98	**UBC SALA: Social Sustainability in Practice** by Melissa Higgs

102	**UniverCity Childcare**	BURNABY BC
126	**Jasper Place Library**	EDMONTON AB
152	**Mill Woods Library**	EDMONTON AB

174	**Appendix**

Foreword: The Contours of Public Life
Christopher Macdonald

Images from André Kertész' book *On Reading*.
OPPOSITE LEFT Greenwich Village, N.Y.C., June 19, 1966
OPPOSITE RIGHT Park Avenue, N.Y.C., June 8, 1963
THIS PAGE Paris, 1928

"An invite to the porch is not an invite to the house. Its terms are limited to a brief visit on the porch, no refreshments necessarily provided unless the occupants have such at hand."[1]

When we talk about public places—and we continue to do so regularly—we often presume that there is an absolute threshold beyond which 'publicness' is formed. The truth is that the transformation from 'private' to 'public' is much more graduated and subtle. Commentators have distinguished an arena of 'community' life[2] distinct from public life, but I would like to suggest that the gradation could be nuanced further. As preface to observing the following work and as a challenge to our conventional assumptions, I would begin by characterizing a public life delineated by *contour*.

Just as vertical definitions in a contoured portrayal of landscape can frame absolute distinctions—of differing ecologies for instance—at the same time they express a precise sense of gradation. The categorical shift from public to private may of course occur precipitously, but may more often be drawn out across a deliberately cultivated incline. This evocation of landscape helps to reconfigure the question of publicness from a toggle switch of 'off and on' to what is closer to our actual, daily experience of a broad continuum. Private spaces transform to public realms in varied manners. This sense of continuous contours of difference may prove fruitful in understanding how a concern for shared—but not necessarily congruent—values remains central to the design of urban institutions and landscapes.

I would suggest two specific and positive outcomes of this allusion to *contour*. First, it draws attention to qualities of transition as much as it does to spaces set apart and distinct from one another. As designers and as citizens this invitation to the consideration of *threshold* can only contribute to a richer communal life.

Second—and I would say crucial to the consideration of the work presented here— this sense of *contour* encourages a broad and inclusive understanding of the 'public' realm. It allows us to consider the use of social media in consultative prelude to sit alongside the reassuring presence of a fire hall as instruments that together contribute to common understanding and participation. Indeed, it might invite us to consider that in our unabashedly plural and dynamic world, the space that we share is not only public but also truly *cosmopolitan*.[3]

In observing this determined and finely measured body of work, two other related observations come to mind. First, the question of the degree to which a 'public' clientele inevitably privileges the very direct correspondence between design and programme. Is clarity of purpose a necessary outcome arising from public accountability? In a more general context of an architectural culture, is it either essential or even useful for design to be found in the service of cultivating difference and singularity? Is it possible that—and perhaps especially—the exercise of public investment should emphasize the contingent and ultimately resilient qualities of generosity?…the creation of spaces whose sense of purpose is perhaps as much as *elusive* as it is *inevitable*?

What distinguishes the work presented here is its clear sense of participation in a process of ongoing enquiry. This is a practice that is as deliberate in raising questions as it is in pursuing answers—a practice that values the recursive critical consideration that lies at the foundation of all significant architectural production. As such the overview of a lifetime of practice presents an impulse that gives pleasure in and of itself and points to a future of continuing efforts to probe at the responsibilities lodged in the construction of public life.

1. *A Guide to Porch Etiquette* from Garrison Keillor: Lake Wobegon Days, 1985, Viking Press.

2. "*Many people see social relationships as either Private or Public. They don't distinguish an important third form, Community life. Public life is sociability with a diversity of strangers: Community life is sociability with people you know somewhat.*" Michael Brill, *Problems With Mistaking Community Life for Public Life*, Places 14:2.

3. See Kwame Anthony Appiah *Cosmopolitatan Patriots' in Critical Inquiry* 23:3.

Places Manifesto: Life Within Buildings
Darryl Condon, HCMA Managing Principal

"Social activities occur spontaneously, as a direct consequence of people moving about and being in the same spaces. This implies that social activities are indirectly supported whenever necessary and optional activities are given better conditions in public spaces."
—Jan Gehl, from *Life Between Buildings*

In his highly influential book, *Life Between Buildings* (originally published in 1971), Jan Gehl demonstrated a compelling need for architects and urban planners to design spaces that support and encourage the wide range of social interactions that are critical to a healthy community. It was written at a time when the disastrous results of post-war modernist city planning were being felt, and the need to challenge the pervasive thinking of the day was becoming clear. Together with colleagues such as William H. Whyte and Jane Jacobs, his thinking has been central to re-thinking how cities are designed. Gehl, Whyte, and Jacobs focused on the spaces between buildings and in fact argued that this was far more important than what happened within the buildings that defined these spaces. Our philosophy is not necessarily at odds with this opinion but rather looks to extend this thinking. It is our view that the next step in the evolution of city-making is to extend the principles, now widely accepted by urban planners, to the spaces within buildings. It is framed by a belief that the informal activities that Gehl strives to encourage, in the public realm, are also vitally important when they occur within buildings. This premise provides an appropriate introduction to this book which explores the potential for a wide range of public building types to support a broader goal of community building. It is the consistent focus on the social potential of life within buildings that is the common thread explored here.

This book, which features a variety of public buildings designed by our firm, HCMA Archtiecture + Design, is a companion to our earlier book: *Pools: Aquatic Archiecture*. The underlying philosophy and design priorities are shared both by the projects within the earlier book and by the public buildings that are contained within this volume. As with *Pools*, the projects within *Places* are the result of several decades of an iterative exploration of public building types, with each successive design informed by the public experience of those that preceded them. Through this progression we have recognized convergence within the wide range of public building types and the shared potential that each possesses. Along the way, the notion that public facilities can, and should, help transform communities has shaped our work and led to national and international recognition for the results.

Following is a summary of our principles—as designers serving the community—for shaping public architecture:

1. **All public buildings have a role to play.**
   Regardless of the programmatic functions they house, all public buildings have the potential to serve a broader public mandate. While the capacity varies between building types, it is our responsibility, as architects, to consider the full range of what is possible and to provide responses that maximize the social potential.

2. **Every site and situation is unique.**
   All projects must be carefully situated in response to both their social and their urban/environmental contexts. As designers we must look—to see the potential of a street, outlook, or natural setting—but we must also listen—to hear the real and not just apparent needs of users and clients. Visual insight married to social appropriateness resonates beyond site boundaries, informing design as a catalyst for positive community change.

3. **Involve the community in decision making.**
   The social potential of a public building is enhanced by the level of community involvement that is utilized in the processes associated with their design, construction, and operation. A strong commitment to meaningful community engagement at all stages of a project's life cycle is critical to success.

4. **Design for life.**
   As architects we have a unique ability, and responsibility, to positively influence all stages of life. In an individual person's life, the stages are seamless. The same is true for a community. Truly public buildings accommodate all regardless of ability, race, or beliefs. We create architecture that reduces barriers to use—whether physical, cultural, or social.

5. **Seize opportunities for social space.**
   Informal social space is often overlooked in community facilities. We believe the provision for a variety of these spaces ensures that a building integrates with the lives of its users, and that connections fostered there can benefit all. In planning public facilities, we actively seek opportunities to provide such spaces, large and small, both within and between mandated program elements.

6. **Innovate.**
   Our work is animated by a spirit of innovation. We look for new solutions to the challenges that other designers accept as pre-determined or givens. Pushing boundaries sometimes involves greater risks which need to be managed with careful study, evaluation, testing, and insight.

7. **Learn and evolve.**
   We strive to learn from past projects, both our own and those of others. We learn from what has worked well and from what could be better. We travel and study culturally unique approaches to public architecture from around the world, then seek opportunities to integrate them into our work. Learning is a crucial component of design and building.

8. **Delight and surprise users.**
   We embrace an approach to public architecture that recognizes the need to provide spaces that inspire, engage, and delight their users. We use a variety of timeless design strategies that include bold colour, dynamic views, powerful visual forms, and elements of surprise to provide memorable experiences that bring people back time and time again

9. **Maintain focus on the community.**
   Underlying our work is a belief in a dedicated responsibility to the communities we serve. This means providing facilities that go beyond merely meeting programmatic needs to, instead, define true community places, attractive to all.

Our work is not done in isolation but rather in collaboration with our clients, our staff, our consultants, and the communities where we work. Together we strive to create places that realize Gehl's notion of space that supports social activities, and to design buildings that play a significant role in shaping our communities. For this we are very grateful.

Toward Social Sustainability
Jim Taggart

"The public realm is the place where citizens can meet as equals; it is the place where societies build trust."
—Alexandros Washburn,
Chief Urban Designer, City of New York

The Public Realm

New York is famous for the vitality of its street life, a phenomenon much celebrated in Jane Jacobs's seminal work of the early 1960s *The Death and Life of Great American Cities*. Jacobs wrote at length on the "ballet of Hudson Street"—the choreography of daily comings and goings of the many and varied people who lived and worked in her particular corner of Lower Manhattan.

For the first time, Jacobs put forth the argument that these seemingly trivial daily interactions—were in fact a kind of glue that held the community together. Indeed, if asked to describe their community, most residents of Lower Manhattan would speak first of these casual but cordial relationships before they would speak of the historic brownstone buildings, Battery Park, or their proximity to the river.

Jacobs recognized the value of the social, economic, and demographic diversity of her neighbourhood, and of the 'fine grained mix of residential, commercial, and other uses that made up its physical fabric. She was also among the first to recognize the negative social impacts of the major infrastructure projects planned for Lower Manhattan and elsewhere by the powerful freeway proponent Robert Moses.

Such projects were a legacy of Le Corbusier's early 20th century vision of the 'Ville Radieuse'—a mechanistic approach to city planning that sought to replace human-scaled, pedestrian-oriented streets with multi-lane arterial roads, and old but much beloved, ground-oriented housing with formulaic high rise apartments set in fields of green. The implicit assumption was that these strategies, by virtue of their Modernity alone, would improve the well-being of the people whose lives they touched. With the benefit of hindsight, we can now say that in most cases the reverse has proven to be true.

New York is rare, if not unique among cities in the New World, in having a critical mass of dense mixed-use buildings in its urban core, and both a street network and subterranean public transit system that predates the mass production of affordable automobiles. As such, the day to day functioning of the city was less affected than most by the wholesale removal of streetcar systems that occurred in many North American cities in the mid-20th century.

The beneficial legacy of this situation is a public realm that continues to be used, enjoyed, and valued by everyone. This appreciation of public space is much more common in historic cities of the Old World, which developed at a time when public life was critical to the functioning of society, and indeed to daily subsistence.

The rapid growth of cities over the last two centuries has been paralleled (and in some respects driven) by equally rapid growth in transportation and communications technology. As populations have become more numerous, they have also become more dispersed. Satellite towns and suburbs first connected to their urban cores by trams and trolleys are now leap frogged by multi-lane arterial roads and highways that penetrate ever further into the vanishing rural landscape.

This model of urban development, first promoted in the immediate post-World War II period on the promise of individual land ownership for every family, proved so compelling that in less than half a century it transformed the continent. Thus, far more common in North America than Jacobs' high density mixed-use neighbourhood in Lower Manhattan, are sprawling, low density cities like Los Angeles, Houston, or Phoenix. In these examples, large tracts of land are separated by municipal ordnances into residential, commercial, industrial, and other exclusive-use zones.

In purely physical terms, the result has been the creation of a public realm (and I hesitate even to use that term) that is vast, barren, ill-defined, and inaccessible. In a built environment designed for cars, there are a number of negative implications for people.

In the absence of a meaningful public

OPPOSITE PAGE AND LEFT The Sixth Estate is a mixed use development in the Fairview Slopes neighbourhood of Vancouver BC. The open space plan includes a pedestrian walkway that traverses the site, and a series of intimate courtyards sheltered from the adjacent arterial road by glass block walls. The buildings wrap around the courtyards and over the walkway creating a hierarchy of spatial experience and multiple opportunities for interaction between residents and business owners.

realm, the city tends to become commodified and corporatized. Main Street, which in the past was a public place to which everyone had the democratic right of access, has become The Mall where corporate interests prevail, and from which certain sectors of society are routinely excluded. As typologies, shopping malls are almost invariably inward looking, isolated from any kind of public thoroughfare by asphalt parking lots.

When this typology is repeated everywhere, in strip malls, big box stores, business parks, and elsewhere, walking is discouraged. Not only does this eliminate any sense of connection between the individual and the public realm, but over time, this form of development has also been demonstrated to have a negative impact on public health. For example the Toronto Diabetes Atlas, published in 2007, showed a strong correlation between low density areas of the city where residents had limited access to retail services and public transit, with elevated levels of diabetes and other chronic health conditions.

The negative effects are not just physical however. In automobile-oriented environments, both the quantity and quality of social interaction diminishes. These dispersed (low density) communities increase our physical isolation, while rapidly evolving electronic communications technology provides us with the illusion of independence and autonomy. Today, with an ever increasing proportion of interaction between people taking place in the virtual rather than the physical domain, face to face social interaction is now something that we have the discretion to engage in or not.

However, research confirms that making the latter choice can have profoundly negative psychological and physiological consequences. Since prehistory, humans have been hard wired to find comfort in communion with others on whom they have relied for food, shelter, and protection. Without that physical association, our production of stress hormones increases and simultaneously the effectiveness of our immune system diminishes. This leaves us vulnerable to anxiety and depression as well as a wide range of physical ailments.

So what is to be done to make our cities healthier and more socially sustainable? This book provides a primer for architectural practitioners and the public alike; a portfolio of projects completed by a firm that, over its 40 year history has devoted much of its creative energy to the enhancement of the public realm. Whether streets, squares, or buildings, these projects are "places" in the architectural sense—public spaces where people want to be, where they can meet and mingle on equal terms, and (as Alexandros Washburn would put it) "build trust."

Schools, libraries, and community centres are the focal public buildings in most communities. In today's secular, multi-ethnic societies they assume a symbolic importance equivalent to that of religious buildings in the past, and foster the same relationships as Jane Jacobs observed in the streets of Manhattan. They are the "social glue" of contemporary society and the underpinning of community resilience.

Making Places

Roger Hughes started his Vancouver practice, a predecessor to HCMA Architecture + Design, with the aim of creating architecture that would serve the needs of its community. Experience gained on social housing projects while a graduate student at the Architectural Association in London, England nurtured a nascent interest in public architecture and affirmed his belief that the quality of the public realm has a direct bearing on the quality of community life.

Hughes returned to Vancouver in the early 1970s, where by chance a new piece of legislation had just been introduced. For the first time, the Condominium Act permitted the construction of projects with common ownership, which gave Hughes' UK experience immediate market value and led to the design of the firm's first landmark project, the Sixth Estate housing development on Vancouver's Fairview Slopes.

So began a series of projects informed by their greater physical context, and embodying a concern for the enhancement of the public realm. This trajectory influenced the work of the firm as it evolved over the next four decades.

RIGHT At Rogers Elementary School in Victoria, BC, classrooms are clustered to give definition to the central "resource spine". The articulation of this common area encourages learning in a variety of styles and group sizes. BELOW Students have named the central circulation spine of the Duchess Park Secondary School in Prince George, BC, "the Canyon". The social armature around which the remainder of the program is organized, it is naturally lit with a variety of meeting places and views into and out of the school.

FAR LEFT While fixed program areas are sheltered behind opaque walls, flexible social spaces are carved out of the rectangular form and revealed to the outside world through large expanses of glazing. LEFT The Building Blocks Playhouse is an exercise in opportunity. While traditional playground equipment offers children a range of specific activities, it limits their options for contemplation and collaboration. In contrast, Building Blocks provides a variety of spatial experiences that in turn lead to more creative and self-directed play.

What distinguishes HCMA's design approach from that of most other contemporary architects is its conceptual shift from the traditional departure points of form or function, to a more organic and humanist approach by which inhabitation of the building and its surroundings mediates between these often opposing forces.

While function implies an empirical definition of purpose, and form a pre-occupation with sculptural abstraction, inhabitation connotes an understanding that buildings should embrace the richness and diversity of the human experience.

This conceptual thread is traceable through several iterations of the practice and continues to be the central theme of the more current work featured in this book, whether that be the earlier work created under Hughes' direction, or that of the firm's current partners Darryl Condon, Karen Marler, Stuart Rothnie, or Carl-Jan Rupp.

Thirty years on, the Sixth Estate remains a touchstone for the firm. Completed in 1981, the project occupies fully half a city block on a north facing slope that borders an arterial road. The scheme focused on the creation of a hierarchy of open space, protected from traffic noise, above which the majority of the condominium units could benefit from city and mountain views. Three street front buildings of concrete construction were retained, and between them small courtyards developed behind high glass block walls. An east-west pedestrian path traverses the site, from which steps lead down to the courtyards and up to the condominiums.

Commercial office spaces in the renovated structures have their front doors on this path, while the larger apartment units bridge over it, creating a sense of entry and identity for each courtyard cluster.

The primacy of social space is a recurring theme in HCMA's work, both as an organizer of program and a generator of form. Because of the intensely vehicle-oriented nature of the immediate context, this project had to create its own public realm. The open space concept was the most important driver of design, with the architectural program manipulated so as to reinforce the quality and definition of these social spaces.

Although separated by more than three decades and more than 500 miles, a similar response can be seen in HCMA's latest project, the Mill Woods Library, Seniors Centre, and Multi-Cultural Facility in Edmonton, AB, under construction in 2014. Here, amid the monotony of suburban malls, Mill Woods also creates its own context. By introducing a new architectural syntax to the neighbourhood, the project engages in a critical dialogue with the surrounding buildings.

Internally, the Mill Woods project manifests an approach to spatial relationships that HCMA refers to as 'tight packed, loose fit', in which other program elements are used to articulate and define the social spaces in the building. This particular approach to space-planning can be traced back to the firm's first school project, Rogers Elementary completed in 1991.

The school, located in Saanich, BC, was the winning entry in a rare open competition for a public building in British Columbia. Located adjacent to the sensitive ecosystem of Christmas Hill Park, the building adheres to a carefully conceived 'great circle' campus plan, delicately placed within a natural wooded setting. The school provides a variety of instructional and other spaces scaled to different group sizes and learning formats. The classroom blocks are pushed together to define a linear resource spine that acts as an extension for each classroom and encourages unrestricted use of the resource centre. Exposed structure lifts the dynamic roof planes free of the solid masonry volume below, their dramatic cantilevers extending the influence of the building into the surrounding landscape.

In the past two decades, information technology has revolutionized education at every level, and HCMA's work has evolved to maintain its position at the leading edge of practice. In secondary and post-secondary environments, the delivery model has moved from the classroom with the instructor as the main conduit for learning, to a more flexible and dispersed model in which collaborative learning takes place wherever there is a wireless internet signal.

Completed in 2010, Duchess Park Secondary School in Prince George, BC (Page 46), manipulates a standard Ministry of Education program to provide a hierarchy of interconnected social spaces of varied character arranged along a central "skylit circulation canyon."

BELOW The UniverCity Childcare Centre in Burnaby, BC, facilitates the experiential learning opportunities advocated by the Reggio Emilia education program. Within the building there are spaces of varying scale and character formed by the explicit use of natural materials. Large windows extend the learning experience to the community beyond.

Careful attention to materiality, natural light, and views gives these spaces, and the entire school, a feeling of quality more usually associated with a college campus. Remarkably, this is a design/build project whose success has led to similar commissions for Royal Bay and Oak Bay secondary schools on Vancouver Island.

Pre-school and elementary level education has been less profoundly affected by information technology, but there is an increased emphasis on experiential and collaborative learning. At the UniverCity Childcare Centre in Burnaby, BC, completed in 2012 (Page 102), a compact core of service spaces creates an armature around which a variety of learning and social spaces are arranged, and creates the opportunity for a mezzanine that overlooks them all. Spatially dynamic, the architecture encourages a spirit of enquiry and exploration that resonates with the Reggio Emilia philosophy of early childhood education that the centre embraces.

This same spirit carries through to the design of the Building Blocks playhouse (Page 88), part of a limited design competition that took place in 2012. HCMA's entry departs from the carefully orchestrated sequences of physical play dictated by conventional play equipment, in favour of a variety of spatial experiences that open the imagination to multiple possibilities.

If the revolution in information technology has had a profound effect on education, then its impact on the design of public libraries has been transformative—to the extent that it merits

a separate and more comprehensive essay elsewhere in this book.

The firm's first library was completed in 1993 and is located on the south edge of Renfrew Park on Vancouver's east side. Renfrew was the first in a new generation of branch libraries that emphasized public accessibility and community use. The building fronts onto 22nd Avenue, creating a strong civic presence with its dramatic projecting roof and small public piazza with views through the park to the mountains.

As with many HCMA projects, the form and organization of the building draws on its landscape context, in this case a solid, vine-covered concrete base rising like a rock from the verdant slope. Continuous perimeter windows accentuate the lightness of the roof structure. The building reinforces the "desire lines" that traverse the park, connecting the entrance piazza via a long sloping path to the existing community centre, and back to the parking garage tucked into the hill below the library.

Renfrew Library was completed shortly before the arrival of the internet and therefore provides an interesting point of comparison for the projects that followed.

Completed in 2008, Whistler Public Library in Whistler, BC (Page 28), still has some program elements in common with Renfrew: substantial numbers of traditional book stacks, meeting rooms accessible for community use after hours and an entrance piazza that announces the public nature of the building.

On more detailed investigation however we find more dedicated, yet flexible social space, including a community "living room" (with lounge seating and a fieldstone fireplace) that provides a welcome, admission-free meeting place for Whistler's many seasonal workers.

Jasper Place Library in Edmonton, AB (Page 126), was completed in 2012, and further develops the theme of social space to the extent that traditional library components no longer appear as fixed program elements. Rather, they are flexible, adaptable, and positioned so as to define and delineate the primary social spaces.

Beyond Place

To my knowledge, Jane Jacobs never used the term "social sustainability", but in today's parlance that was exactly what she was writing about: the idea that a community is defined and sustained by the social relationships it fosters, and that its resilience depends on the understanding and respect of its diverse members for one another.

In the 1960s, the resolve of the community was tested by the highway proposals of Robert Moses, and the citizens of Lower Manhattan ultimately proved equal to the task. Their success demonstrated a strength of character we would now refer to as "resilience"—a quality that is increasingly in demand in the face of new and future threats.

In October of 2012, some 50 years after the publication of *The Death and Life of Great American Cities*, Jane Jacobs' old neighbourhood was one of the area's most severely affected by Hurricane Sandy. In fact, Lower Manhattan was the subject of a mandatory evacuation order proclaimed by Mayor Michael Bloomberg in the face of the oncoming storm.

Throughout New York City, the damage and disruption caused by Sandy was significant. The subway was shut down because of flooding, and all but one of the tunnels connecting Manhattan to the outside world were also closed. Lower Manhattan south of 26th Street lost its power supply and the New York Stock Exchange, the economic heart of the nation, was forced to suspend operations for 48 consecutive hours. For two nights, the only illumination on the streets of Lower Manhattan came from the flashing lights of emergency service vehicles.

Across New York State thousands of homes were destroyed by wind, water, or fire; an estimated 250,000 cars were damaged beyond repair. Six thousand people were evacuated from their homes in Midtown Manhattan following a crane collapse on a building site, and across the city there were 53 storm related deaths. The estimated cost of the damage was $18 billion, and at the time of writing repairs are still underway. All this is to confirm that things have changed, and we must turn our attention to creating communities that will be resilient in the face of the new pressures and uncertainties that climate change will bring.

The future-proofing of physical infrastructure is one aspect of resilience: New York City held

RIGHT As evidence of a new adaptive approach to sustainability, the River District Experience Centre in Vancouver BC sits above the flood plain of the adjacent Fraser River. Designed as a temporary sales and visitor facility, the River District Experience Centre has become the social hub of the nascent community.

a competition to redesign and raise its subway grates above the level of projected future flood, and is considering legislation to ensure all electrical and mechanical service equipment in new buildings is installed above ground.

On the other side of the equation is the human factor. Social sustainability is no longer simply about human health and well-being—it is now about the strength and flexibility (and may ultimately be about the survival) of our communities. Nurturing social relationships, mutual respect, and a sense of common purpose is now a high stakes game.

In coastal communities, more frequent and more severe storm events bring with them the increased likelihood of tidal surges and flooding; and the prospect of an overall rise in sea levels has even more profound implications. In the City of North Vancouver, BC, HCMA is involved in a major infrastructure project in which protecting the community from the effects of sea level rise is a primary design consideration.

This same concern has begun to influence the programming and design of individual buildings. On the North Arm of the Fraser River in Vancouver, the River District Experience is a temporary visitor centre for a new residential community. Not surprisingly, the program includes a display space where multimedia messaging promotes the sustainable attributes of the neighbourhood. More surprising (and more compelling) is the inclusion of community amenities: a 50-seat restaurant that buzzes unceasingly with locals and visitors alike; and a multi-purpose space behind the display boards that is regularly taken over for yoga classes and preschool story time. Lifted above the 100-year flood plain, the River District Experience embraces all aspects of social sustainability.

In regard to buildings that address the new realities of community resilience, HCMA has recently been commissioned to design emergency services facilities that can also serve as post-disaster information and operations centres. HCMA has infused these projects with the same sensibility toward social sustainability that informs its other public projects.

Included in this book is the Steveston FireHall in Richmond, BC (page 75). Completed in 2012, the innovative design brings a new level of openness and transparency to this landmark building type.

Further representative of its commitment to social sustainability, HCMA has developed a new course for the University of British Columbia's School of Architecture and Landscape Architecture. Emphasizing the growing importance of this subject, Darryl Condon's course summary opens with the following quotation from Andrew Ross' book *Bird on Fire*:

> Today, it is the task of averting drastic climate change that might be described as an experiment – a vast social experiment in decision-making and democratic action.

Success in that endeavor will not be determined primarily by large technological fixes, though many will be needed along the way. Just as decisive to the outcome is whether our social relationships, cultural beliefs, and political customs will allow for the kind of changes that are necessary. That is why the climate crisis is as much a social as a biophysical challenge, and why the solutions will have to be driven by a fuller quest for global justice than has hitherto been tolerated or imagined.

As we move forward into more uncertain times, the work of HCMA Architecture + Design continues to offer leadership and inspiration. In our efforts to create resilient communities and achieve social sustainability, the projects in this book have much to offer planners, architects, and others across North America and throughout the world.

From Temples of the Mind to the People's Temple
The Changing Role of Public Libraries
by Darryl Condon

OPPOSITE PAGE   The Library of Celsius at Ephesus, Turkey

In the pantheon of public building types, the library is the most dynamic in terms of its changing role and the physical manifestations that support it. The shift in library design priorities, from a long period of stability to an era of continual evolution, mirrors the societal transformations of the information age. Many have speculated that with the advent of the internet and information technology public libraries would cease to be relevant, but in reality public library usage continues to increase. The public often speak with their feet. The forces of change that are transforming usage necessitate a re-thinking of the physical structure of our libraries, and we, as a practice, have been exploring the social and spatial implications of this both through our work and through our research. In order to place in context the future of the public library, both as a building type and its social role, it is useful to examine the history of how the conventional use and practice have evolved.

Founded in the 3rd century BCE by Ptolemy I Soter, and conceived as a repository for all of the world's knowledge, the Bibliotheca Alexandrina was in a sense the "Internet" of the ancient world. From the city at the mouth of the Nile, scholars set forth to the furthest points of the Greek empire, from the Adriatic to the Indus, returning with hand written texts that would be copied at the library's scriptorium. Over decades and even centuries, the collection grew to more than 700,000 papyrus scrolls, equivalent in today's terms to 100,000 books – which can be accommodated on the average smart phone.

Although referred to as a library, the Bibliotheca Alexandrina was much more than a book repository. Because its collection was vast and many of its scrolls unique, it became a meeting point for scholars from many countries. As such, the library was a prototype for what in later centuries would become the university campus. It contained not only the collection itself, for the first time catalogued by subject, but also meeting rooms, lecture halls, and residential accommodation for visiting scholars and researchers. Among those who spent time at the library were Euclid and Archimedes. According to Ismael Seragelbin, Director of the Contemporary Bibliotheca Alexandrina:

> "Members of that remarkable community of scholars mapped the heavens, organized the calendar, established the foundations of science and pushed the boundaries of our knowledge. They opened up the cultures of the world, and established a true dialogue of civilizations. To this day it symbolizes the noblest aspirations of the human mind, global ecumenism, and the greatest achievements of the intellect."

Implicit in Seragelbin's assessment is the idea that for the ancient Greeks, the advancement of knowledge was a collective endeavour. This is an early recognition of the importance of social interaction in the expansion and dissemination of knowledge. Working together, the keenest minds in philosophy, mathematics, astronomy, and other disciplines would further their understanding of the world and the place of humankind within it.

The Greeks believed that the source of inspiration in the arts, sciences, and literature came from the heavens, specifically the nine goddess daughters of Zeus, known collectively as the "Muses". Perceiving it to be a shrine to knowledge, the name they gave to the Biblioteca Alexandrina was "Temple of the Muses." Although there are no archaeological remains or other records of the building, historians believe that the collection was stored in a structure that resembled a Classical Greek temple with an exterior colonnade and a single interior space lined with shelves. This model, in which the imperatives of the collection determined the structure and organization of the building, was repeated across Asia Minor, first by the Greeks and later by the Romans.

Dating from the 2nd century CE, the Library of Celsius, built by the Romans at Ephesus in modern day Turkey, is the best preserved of the libraries of the Classical Age. As inheritors of the Greek temple model, the Romans raised the building on a plinth of nine steps and articulated the symmetrical facade with columns of the Composite and Corinthian orders. Following the basilica form of other public buildings of the

LEFT Inner void surrounded by collection, Exeter Library
OPPOSITE PAGE Stockholm Public Library

Roman world, the library had three aisles, the central one terminating in a semicircular apse. The colonnaded interior measured 17 x 11 metres and functioned as a single space, with shelves for 12,000 texts – some now inscribed on parchment.

With their sophisticated network of roads and engineering infrastructure, the Romans brought to their provincial cities some of the comforts of Rome itself. The construction of libraries in places such as Ephesus confirms that they were also interested in disseminating and assimilating knowledge throughout the empire. The fall of the Roman Empire in the early 5th century CE saw the loss of many public institutions, including libraries, and (particularly in Western Europe) a fragmentation of the knowledge base so painstakingly acquired over the past centuries.

What records remained were held mostly by religious orders, and throughout the medieval period the Catholic Church used that exclusive knowledge to consolidate its own political power. For several centuries, it resisted the translation of the Bible from Latin – the language of clerics – into the language of the common people. Such translations were eventually completed in the early 15th century CE and, with the invention of the printing press, these translations could be widely distributed.

At much the same time, the flowering of the Italian Renaissance ushered in a new era of cultural development and exchange. Prominent families such as the Medicis and the Forzas, whose fortunes derived from various business ventures, competed with one another to show that they were no longer mere merchants, but sophisticated and cultured members of the intelligentsia. In 16th century Florence, the Medici Pope Clement VII commissioned none other than Michelangelo to design a library to house the family's collection of 15,000 manuscripts and other historic texts.

Known as the Biblioteca Medici Laurenziana, the library was constructed in the cloister of the Basilica of San Lorenzo, in Florence, Italy. The upper level reading room is preceded by a grand, vertically proportioned vestibule most of which is taken up by a sculptural and distinctly mannerist triple flight staircase. The reading room, 45 metres long and 10 metres wide, has rows of benches arranged on either side of a central aisle, and lit by side windows placed within the regular grid of recessed columns. This was a private institution, certainly not available to the average Florentine citizen.

In a similar fashion and grander still was Philip II of Spain's' library at the palace of El Escorial outside Madrid. Designed by Juan de Toledo and Juan Herrera in the late 16th century, it too has a reading room with a central aisle, but in this case the reading desks are flanked by the shelves containing the collection. This 'Long Room' configuration remained popular into the 18th century where it was used again in Thomas de Burgh's magnificent library at Trinity College Dublin. Completed in 1733, the original Long Room was a single storey space with a central aisle flanked by bookshelves. By the mid-19th century, the collection had expanded to the extent that it became necessary to raise the ceiling to create a second storey gallery. The now vaulted space, at almost 65 metres in length, remains one of the most impressive libraries in the world. Here, as in the earlier examples, the books are celebrated and act of collecting defines the spatial characteristics.

The modern public library, with its broader and more inclusive social role, began in England with the passing of the Public Libraries Act in 1850. This was one of many significant social reforms in the mid-19th century, starting with the Factories Act of 1833 and continuing through to the Elementary Education Act of 1870 that introduced free and compulsory education for all children aged five to thirteen. Although the Public Libraries Act gave local authorities the power to create free public libraries, only the largest were able to raise the capital necessary to create new facilities.

Thus the spread of "public" libraries throughout the United Kingdom (and the English speaking world) relied heavily on the generosity of philanthropists like the Scottish-American industrialist Andrew Carnegie. Between 1883 and 1929 Carnegie funded the construction of more than 2,500 public libraries, most in the United Kingdom, the United States, and Canada, but also in other parts of the world. They took many forms and adopted a number of Classical

LEFT Collection shelving studies, Mill Woods Library
OPPOSITE PAGE Seattle Public Library

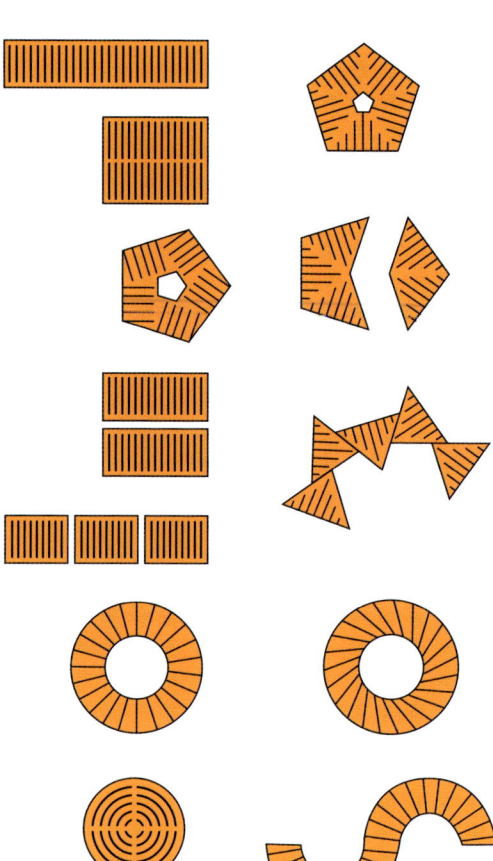

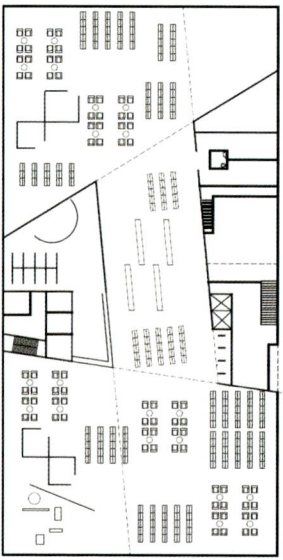

and Revivalist styles according to the taste of the local community, and while the underlying social intention had changed, their form and organization remained tied to their primary function: the storage of books.

Deviations from the rigid rectilinear geometry inherited from the Greeks and Romans were rare, although libraries organized on a circular plan do occur at intervals. Most famous of these is the British Museum Reading Room of 1857, designed by Sidney Smirke, and located in the museum's great court. This became the inspiration for the Canadian Library of Parliament in Ottawa, completed in 1876 to a design by Thomas Fuller and Chillion Jones. This neo-gothic design, a masterpiece of early Canadian design, includes sixteen exterior flying buttresses, a vaulted reading room lined with bookshelves, and features an exposed wood structure and paneling.

Similarly, in the early 20th century, Erik Gunnar Asplund placed a circular reading room at the centre of his Stockholm Public Library. The symmetrical plan with radiating wings was classically inspired, but in the emerging culture of Modernism, he chose to remove the central dome leaving the reading room a flat topped cylinder. Here again, the bookshelves climb the curving walls in a series of tiers, with the collection again defining the main space and the overall identity of the library.

Throughout the 20th century, Modernist libraries were designed like machines for the storage of books. From the physical dimensions of books, and the optimal spacing of book stacks, structural grids were defined and fenestration patterns determined, and from those criteria followed the form. In these buildings, the social spaces are subservient to the needs of the collection and tend to exist in remnant spaces, occupying the zones where the relentless efficiency of the optimal book stack layout is compromised or as a ring around the most efficient shelving. Archetypal among these examples is Louis Kahn's 1972 Exeter Library at Exeter, New Hampshire, in which the plan is a series of three concentric squares that express the different functional spaces. The grand central reading room is flanked by balconies containing book stacks and study carrels. The building has a monumentality and sense of permanence that recalls the libraries of ancient times. Indeed, Kahn himself considered his library a "shrine to knowledge," much as the Greeks had done.

From the conception to the completion of the building, the collection at the Exeter Library had grown significantly, a phenomenon common until the 1980s when the introduction of microfilm made it possible to create copies of documents and greatly reduce the storage space required for certain parts of the collection such as newspapers and journals. This trend has accelerated with digital technology, the Internet, and the availability of e-books. Some predict the eventual disappearance of the book altogether, while others believe that the need

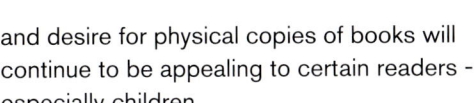

and desire for physical copies of books will continue to be appealing to certain readers - especially children.

Whether a collection ultimately reduces to a fraction of its current size, or disappears altogether, it is clear that the needs of the collection should no longer dictate the architecture of libraries. In more recent projects, such as OMA's Seattle Public Library of 2004, the collection is consolidated to the core of the building, allowing a multitude of social spaces to be arranged loosely around it. This concept is also evident in recent work by Jose Cabanis in Toulouse, France and in Toyo Ito's Sendai Mediatheque in Japan. Likely the most dramatic example of this shifting focus on social spaces is the Rolex Learning Centre in Lausanne Switzerland. Designed by Sanaa, this project consists almost entirely of informal social spaces with the collections seemingly a hindrance to the Architect's preferred use of the space.

The paradox and the possibilities of change are also explored in Sou Fujimoto's Musashino Art University Museum and Library in Tokyo, completed in 2013. Here, Fujimoto takes the key elements of the traditional library, including the books, bookshelves, and the quality of light, and creates a continuous spiral structure of empty bookshelves that completely envelopes the building before extending into the surrounding landscape. While this library still houses a collection of 300,000 volumes, its structure (like that of the Seattle Public Library) is designed

OPPOSITE RIGHT Reading room open to adjacent courtyard, Biblioteca Sant Antoni – Joan Oliver, Barcelona, Spain
OPPOSITE BOTTOM Fluid space below Rolex Learning Centre, Lausanne, Switzerland
BELOW Interconected social spaces, Busan Public Library, Singapore

to accommodate change without destroying the character of the architecture.

The changes in library design are taking place across the globe. While the context may vary, the path of inquiry is universal. We have studied evidence of this in new libraries in countries such as Norway, Holland, Spain, and Singapore, but this is only scratching the surface.

We are also in an era where entire library systems are being renewed and in the process transformed physically, socially, and operationally, with noteworthy examples including City of Seattle and City of Phoenix in the United States and City of Edmonton in Canada. It is in Edmonton that we have had the opportunity to explore the spatial implications of these changes most dramatically.

In our own work, we have moved from the conventional collection driven model as seen in the Renfrew Branch Library of 1993, through the more flexible approach taken in the Whistler Public Library of 2008: where fixed elements of the program are consolidated on the street side of the building; to our most recent work at Jasper Place and Mill Woods in Edmonton: where social spaces are given priority and the remainder of the diminished physical collection occupy the remnant spaces and are then in turn required to define and articulate the social spaces. The central approach recognizes that as the collections reduce the importance of the social spaces remains.

If one were to imagine the ancient Biblioteca Alexandrina with its 700,000 scrolls digitized and stored on a smart phone, there would no doubt be nostalgia at the loss of the sensory aspects of accessing the information: the musty smell of aging scrolls; the anticipation as the librarian searches the shelves for the requested item; and the crackling of the papyrus as it is unrolled. (In fact it is my hypothesis that architects will be among the last to give up the physical artifact of their libraries and I am personally in that camp.) However the desire for knowledge itself and the communal excitement of learning in a truly democratic environment will remain. While we may have exchanged papyrus scrolls for smart phones, libraries will continue to facilitate our quest for knowledge and provide the social environment in which to pursue it. In formal terms, the future structure of libraries may be uncertain, but the continued relevance of the building type is assured for all communities and cultures. The shift in physical needs has and will continue to facilitate an expansion of the social service role, such as was recognized in England in the mid-1800s, and in the process fulfill the larger mandate of all public libraries: to contribute to building citizens and their communities.

Whistler Library
Whistler, BC

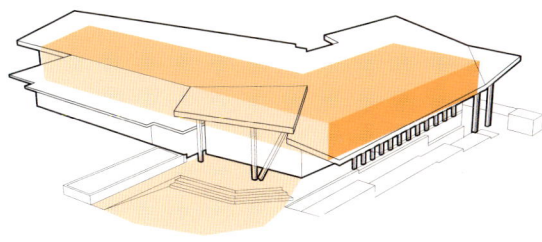

Client
Resort Municipality of Whistler

Year
2007

Size
1,400 m²

Awards
2010 SAB Canadian Green Building Award
2010 Wood Design Award
2009 Lieutenant Governor of BC Award for Architecture
2009 Canadian Wood WORKS! Awards
2009 World Architecture Festival shortlist
2008 Wood Design Real Cedar Award

Nestled in BC's Coast Mountains, and one of the world's premier skiing destinations, the Resort Municipality of Whistler has a resident population of around 10,000. Seasonal workers increase this number to more than 20,000 during the skiing season. Weekenders, who own recreational property in the area, constitute the third significant element of Whistler's unusual demographic. When these weekenders are in residence and tourist accommodation is full, the town can reach a population of 55,000.

The cultural life of the municipality is strongly connected to the environment, and in 2000 Whistler became one of the first municipalities in North America to adopt the "Natural Step program," which strives to maintain the natural balance of the Earth's ecosystems through stewardship of resources and minimizing the negative impact of human activity—strategies dependent on social and economic systems that give individuals the power of choice.

Symbolic of this commitment to sustainability, the new library was designated Whistler's millennium project, a much needed replacement for an aging temporary facility. The library is one of the only truly public spaces in this highly commercialized village and provides a meeting place for many seasonal workers whose personal accommodation may be small and crowded.

The new building occupies a prominent corner location close to Whistler's main pedestrian route known as the "Village Stroll", and mediating between the town, the adjacent park, and distant mountains. To give the building a civic presence on a site that slopes steeply down from Main Street, the L-shaped library structure has been set on a podium that accommodates a parking garage and end of trip bicycle facility. To preserve the views, the remainder of the program has been arranged on a single level with a shallow shed roof.

Low at the entrance lobby, with deep overhangs that shade the south facing windows and create weather protected transitional spaces, the roof rises to the northwest where a window wall connects the reading room to the park beyond and admits abundant natural light. The entrance court becomes a venue for summer festivals and events, extending the reach of the building into the community.

Internally, the two wings of the library are anchored by the "team lounge" and "community living room"—the latter dominated by a large fieldstone fireplace. Here, the mobile book stacks are often wheeled out of the way to create space for public recitals, presentations, and events. Together with the exposed soffit of the solid prefabricated hemlock roof and the wood veneer millwork, the fieldstone elements contribute to the welcoming atmosphere and sense of visual warmth. The gentle rise and fall of the roof and the subtle articulation of interior space create a variety of opportunities for individual or group study or socializing.

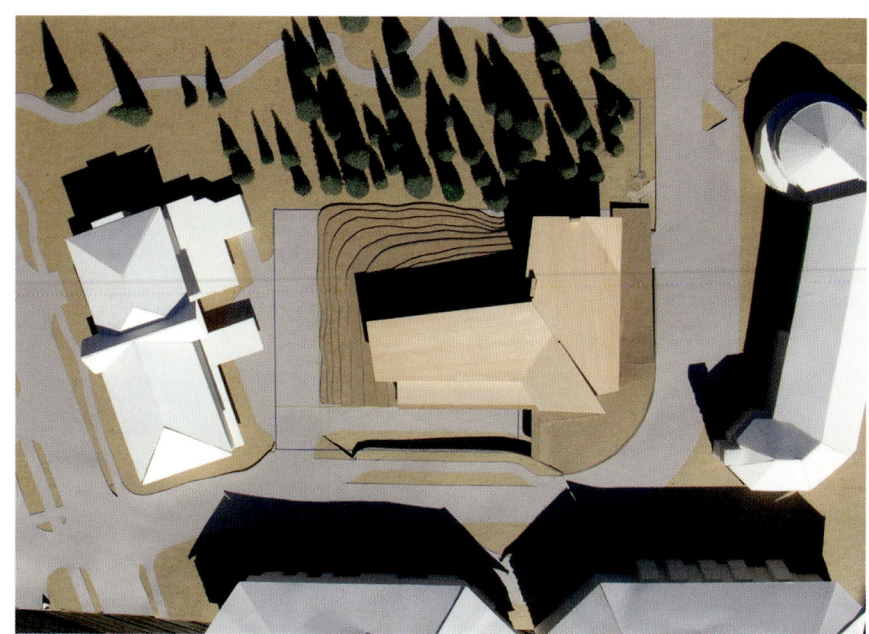

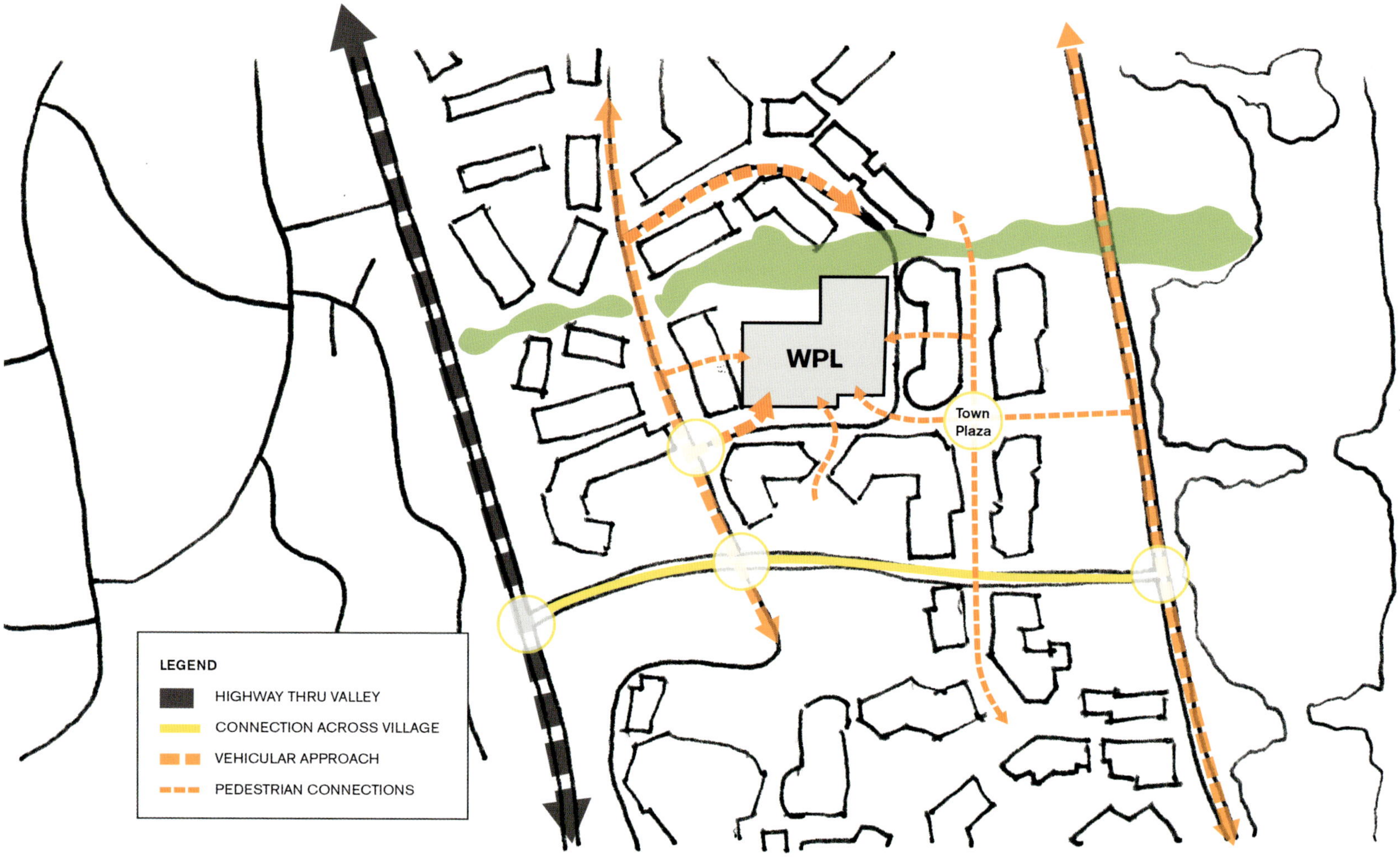
WPL
Town Plaza
LEGEND
HIGHWAY THRU VALLEY
CONNECTION ACROSS VILLAGE
VEHICULAR APPROACH
PEDESTRIAN CONNECTIONS

1 Main Entrance
2 Entry Vestibule
3 Circulation Desk
4 Patron Service
5 Book Drop
6 Workroom
7 Head Librarian Office
8 Copy/Storage
9 Storage
10 Office
11 Staff Room
12 Child Program Room
13 Children's Area
14 Group Study
15 Quiet Carrals
16 Outdoor Reading Terrace
17 Reading Room
18 Fireplace
19 Teen Area
20 Computer Lab
21 Multipurpose Room
22 Arcade

BELOW Expansive glazing on the north facade provides views of the park and creek beyond. A more intimately scaled band extrudes from the facade to create quiet reading carrels.

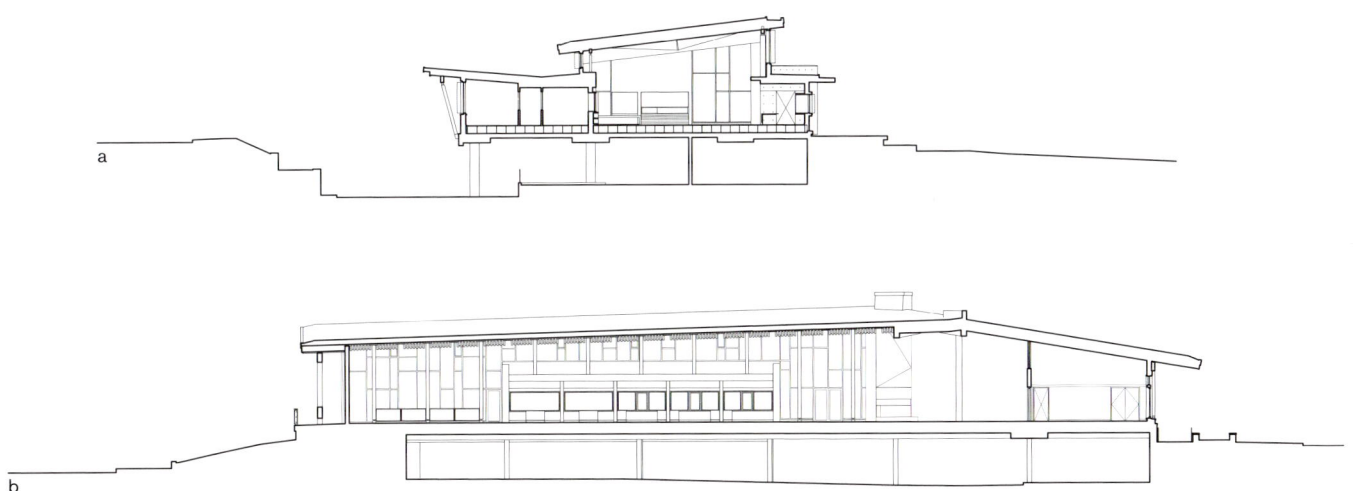

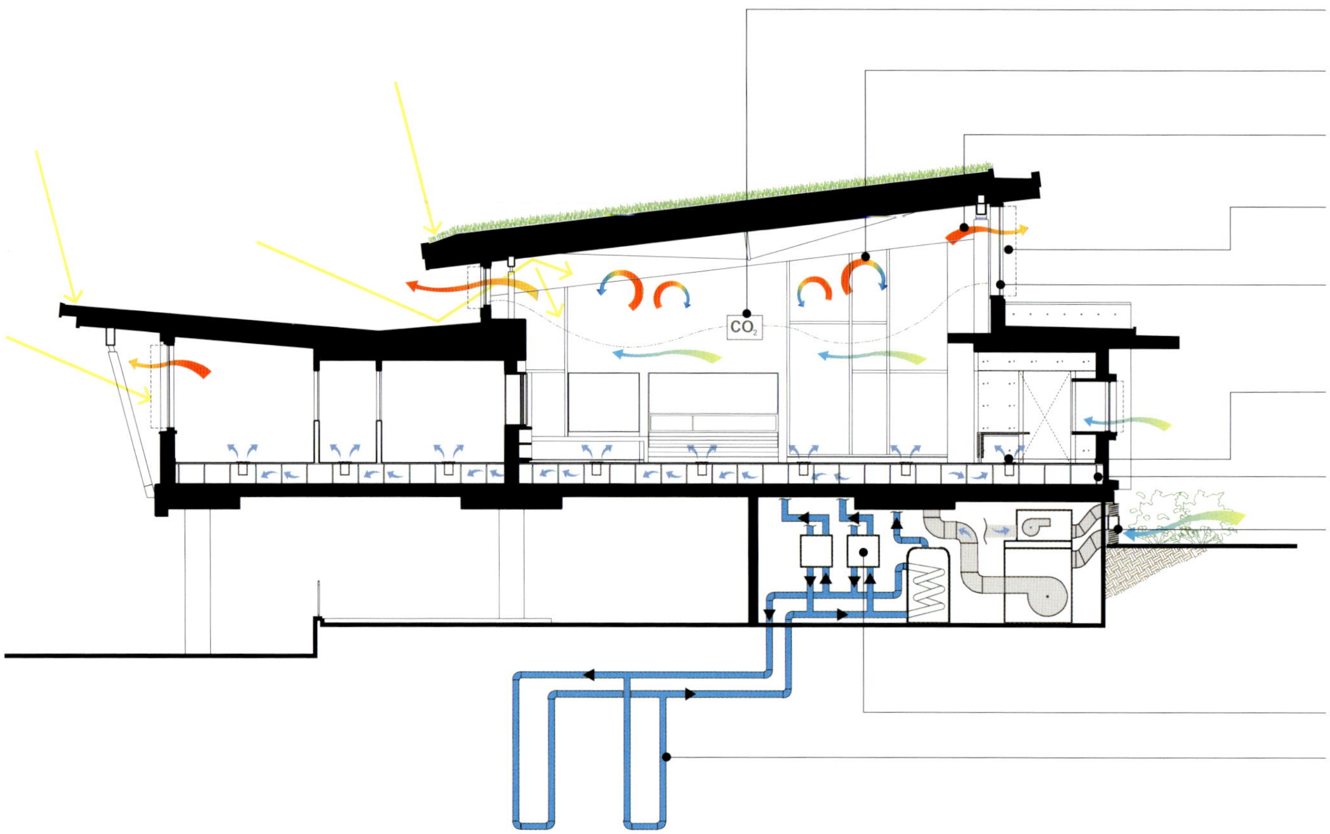

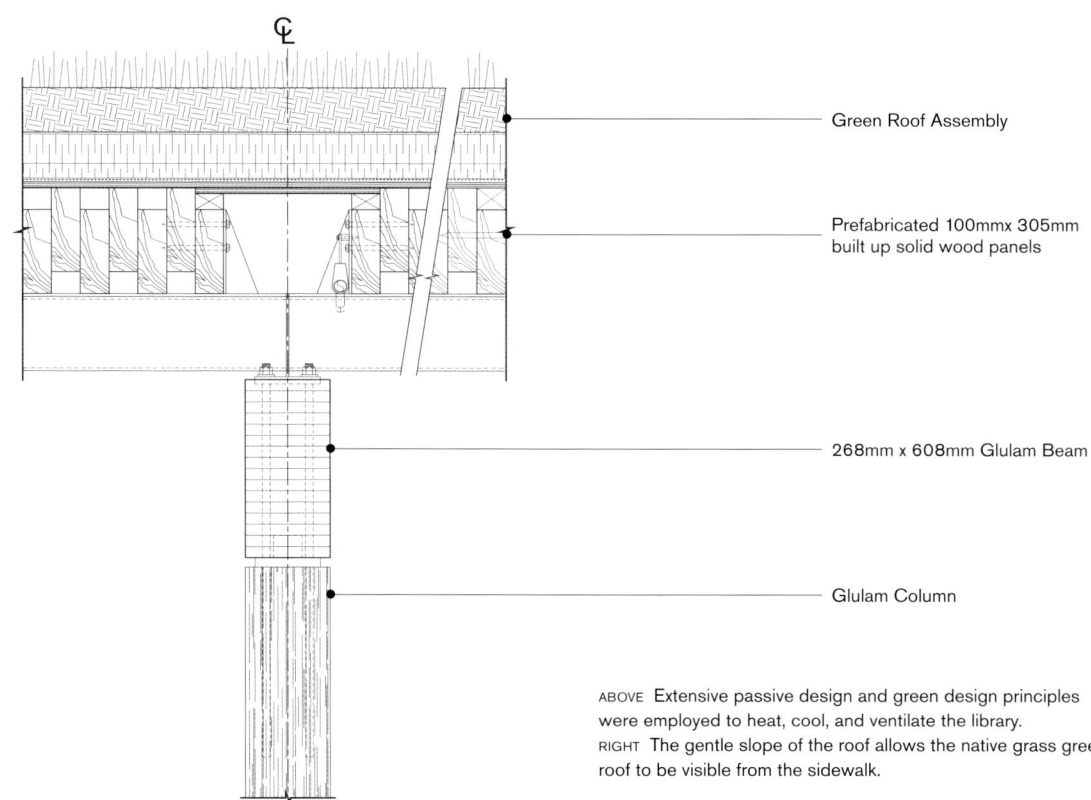

- Ventilation controlled by carbon dioxide sensors
- High level stratified warm air vented/recirculated by control system
- High level heat vented during cooling season
- Large windows allow north light, reducing the need for artificial lightning
- Actuated vents respond to exterior temperatures
- Under floor air distribution with multiple zones for increased control
- High efficiency hot water perimeter heating
- O/A intake from park side of building
- Geothermal heating
- Geothermal loop

- Green Roof Assembly
- Prefabricated 100mm x 305mm built up solid wood panels
- 268mm x 608mm Glulam Beam
- Glulam Column

ABOVE Extensive passive design and green design principles were employed to heat, cool, and ventilate the library.
RIGHT The gentle slope of the roof allows the native grass green roof to be visible from the sidewalk.

ABOVE The innovative prefabricated solid wood panel roof extends from interior to exterior and is visible throughout the space, creating a warm and bright library environment.

WHISTLER LIBRARY

DUCHESS PARK

Duchess Park Secondary School
Prince George, BC

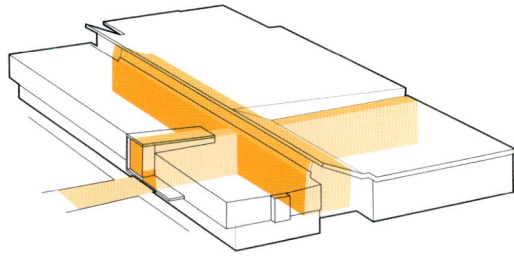

Client
School District No. 57 and School District No. 93

Year
2010

Size
11,040 m²

Awards
2011 Canadian Design-Build Institute Award

Situated in the historic Crescents neighbourhood of Prince George, the largest city in northern British Columbia, Duchess Park Secondary School is HCMA's first school project with a design & build delivery method. A state of the art facility, specifically designed for its extreme climate, Duchess Park is also the province's first LEED Gold certified secondary school.

The two-storey building is home to a diverse educational community of nearly 1,000 students and faculty, who view their physical and social environment as more like a college campus than a traditional secondary school. Recognizing the opportunities inherent in the design/build process, HCMA took a more volumetric approach to the design and detailing. Informal learning spaces are not yet acknowledged or funded within the Ministry of Education's program allocation. Convinced that valuable learning also takes place outside the classroom, HCMA integrated 20% more social space into the building without exceeding the Ministry budget.

The plan is an energy efficient rectangle, bisected along its north-south axis by what the students have called "the Canyon," the primary circulation and social space in the building. A key element of the brief, this multi-purpose atrium space was conceived as a vibrant and versatile social heart for the school. It also acts as an ordering device. Upon arrival, the layout of the public areas is clear. Students, faculty, and guests of all ages quickly feel at home and can find their way intuitively and without direction.

With its hierarchy of scales, the Canyon becomes a meeting place, a forum, a town plaza—a space that promotes and fosters a powerful sense of recognition and identity. As such it supports a vibrant learning community that continues the school's rich tradition of academic and athletic excellence while promoting inclusiveness to all of its students. Among the most successful of these varied spaces are the second floor student benches that overlook 7th Avenue. Small in scale, they nonetheless are key to fostering the community interaction that is fundamental to social sustainability.

The Canyon is flanked on its west side by the Industrial and Fine Arts departments that lie on either side of the gymnasium, and on the east by the two-storey classroom block. Skylights flood the space with natural daylight and bring high levels of borrowed light to internal classrooms. The north end of the Canyon is anchored by the library, while the south end extends to the outdoor student space and bus drop off. The main entrance siting of the school extends a hierarchical urban axial influence east through Duchess Park along 7th Avenue to City Hall and the greater community. This relationship, which was envisioned in Prince George's original "City Beautiful" plan, has reinforced and enhanced existing flows of activity in the community and stimulated the revitalization and development of retail and commercial business in the area. Thus the impact of the building can be felt beyond the boundaries of the site.

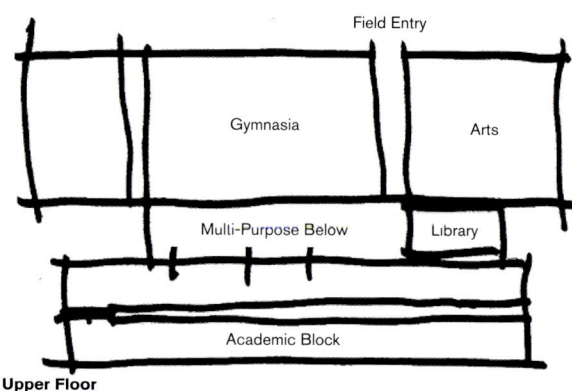
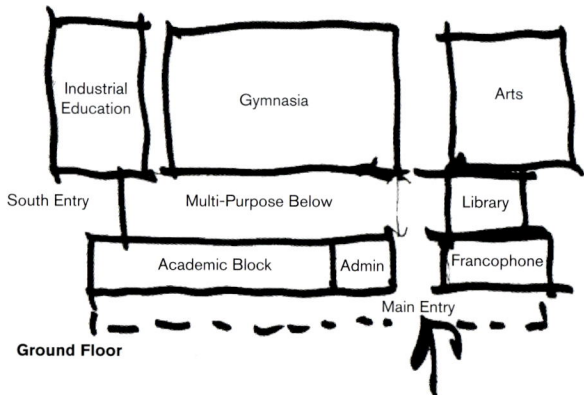
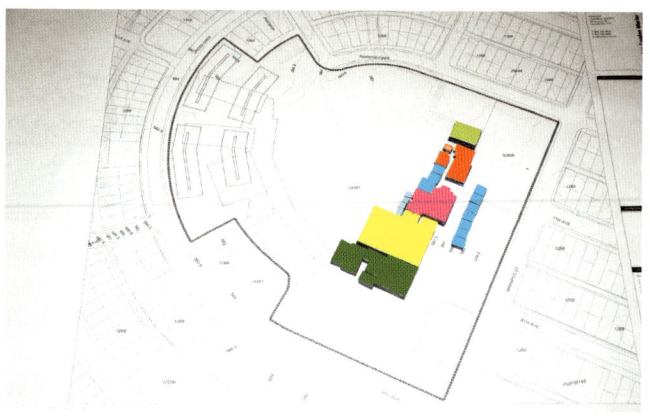
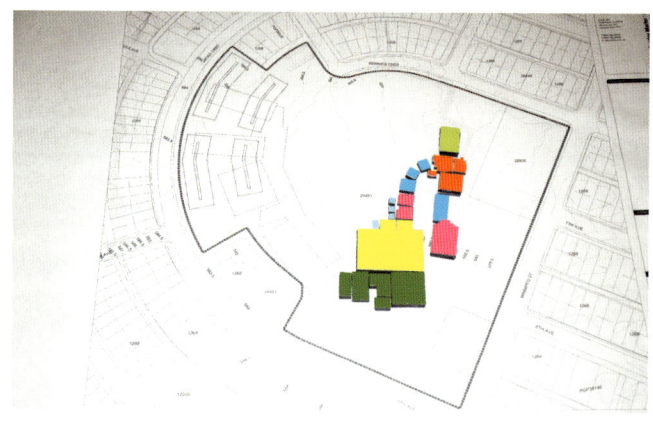

The siting of the school provides a building which fits the end of the hierarchical urban axis along 7th Avenue and connects the school's entrance directly with City Hall. This urban gesture supports engagement between the school and the greater Prince George community.

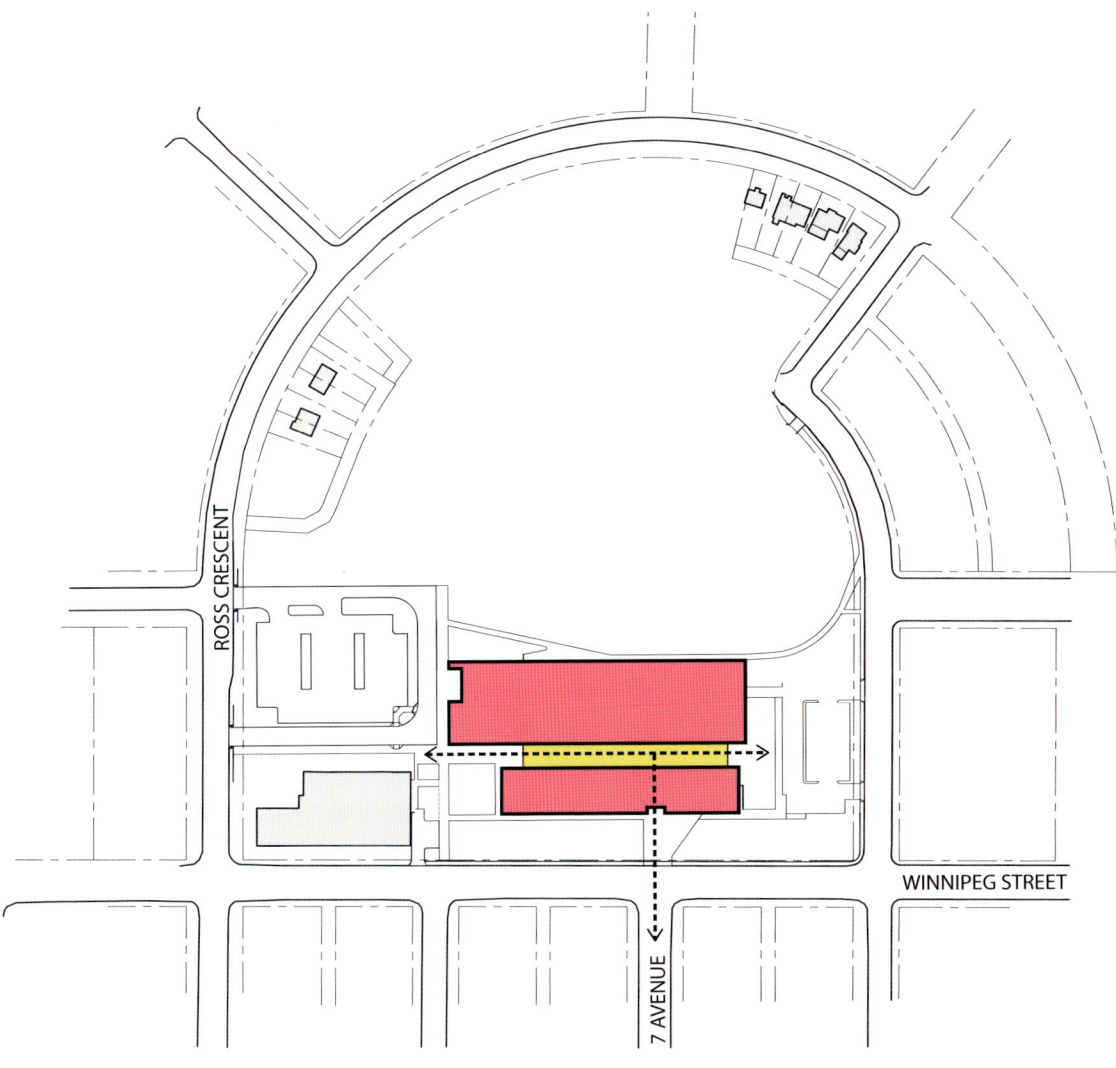

LEFT The Academic spaces are grouped along the East to not only capture the morning daylight but to create a formal frontage to Winnipeg Street that gives the opportunity to express a modern structure that is clearly a school.

The multipurpose atrium and main circulation space creates a clear programmatic heart and gives a spatial identity to the school's philosophy of "Success for All." This student-named Canyon is a meeting place, a forum, a town plaza—a space that promotes and fosters the best sense of recognition and identity and supports a strong and vibrant learning community. The Canyon fosters a sense of belonging, togetherness, and purpose and has reduced problems with marginalization, separation, and vandalism.

Natural, local materials are used in abundance to provide local contextual identity, including an accoustic wood wall in the central circulation space.

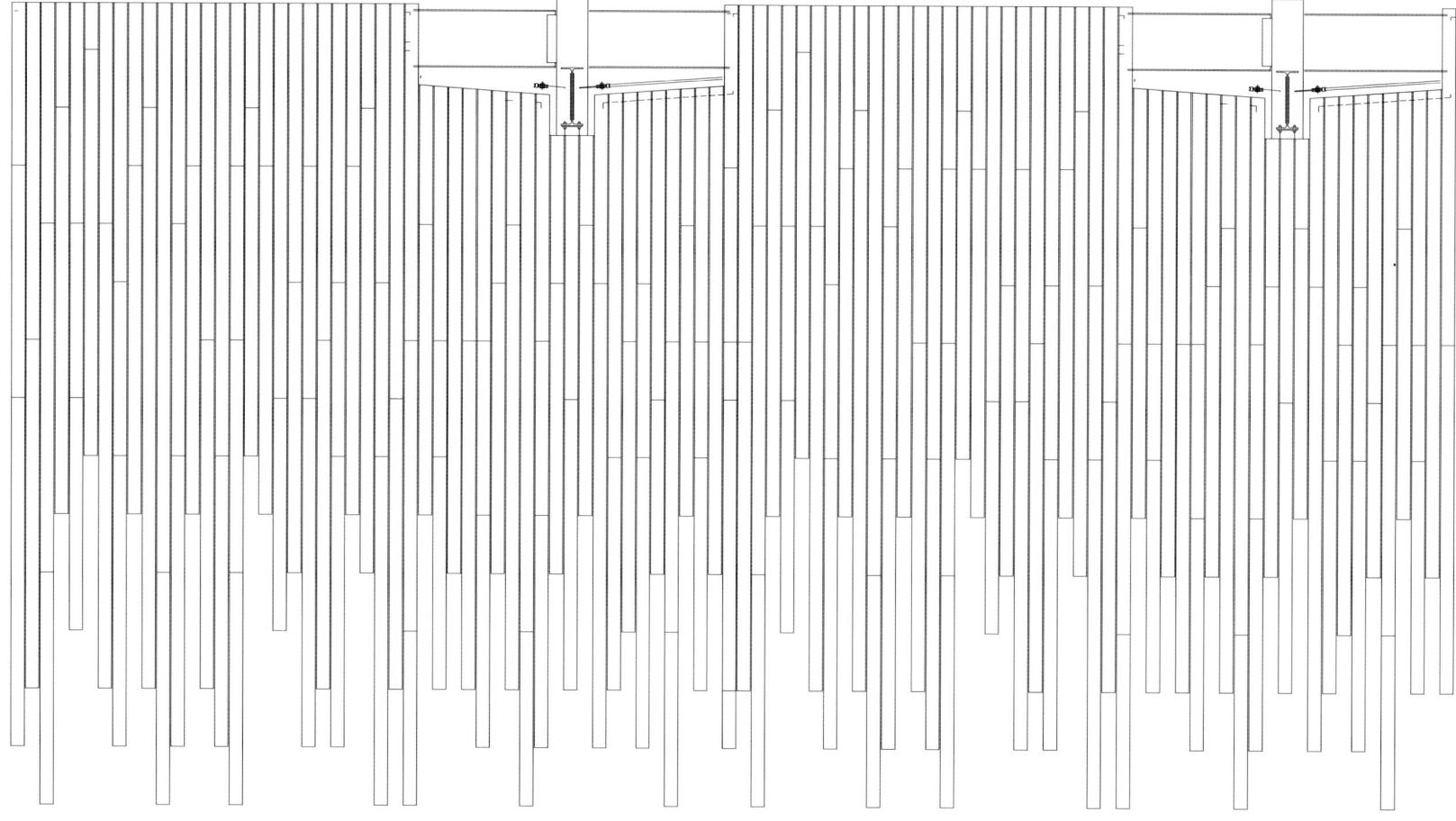

The feature wood wall has many functions. The layout, with varying depth and spacing of individual boards, is designed in conjunction with backing absorptive materials to create an acoustically comfortable gathering place. The feature wall frames a mechanical transfer plenum for internal air displacement, allowing air to filter between the spaced boards from the expansive triple Gymnasium into the Multi-Purpose Room.

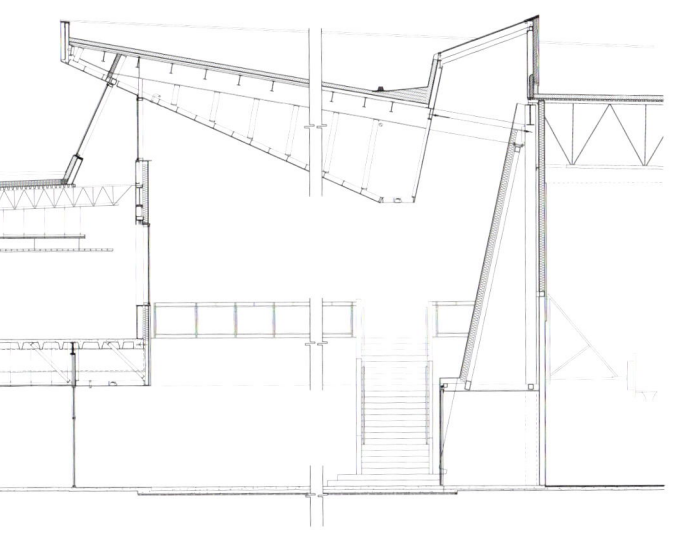

ABOVE The Canyon is crested by a linear skylight which washes the acoustic wood wall with warm natural light.

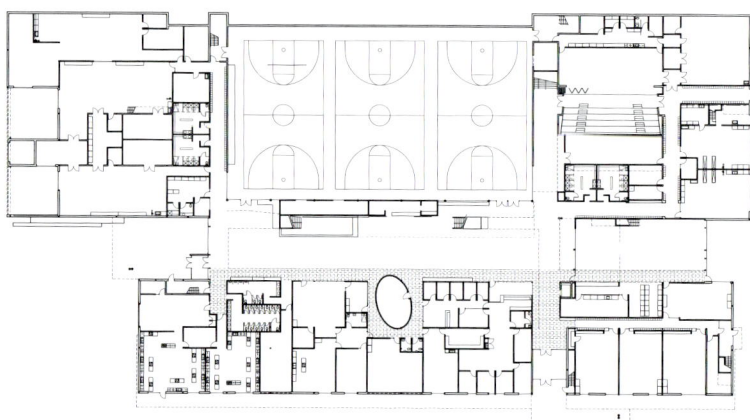

Main floor plan

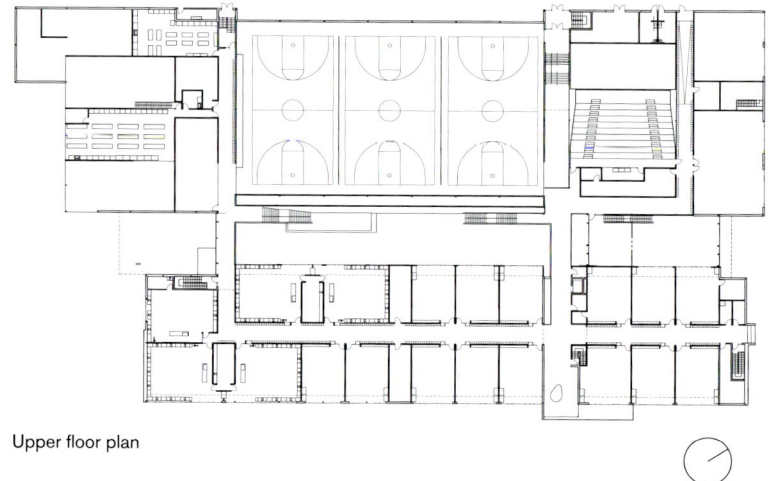

Upper floor plan

RIGHT Clerestory windows and a linear skylight bring daylight deep into the interior-facing classrooms. Windows animate the interior facade of the classroom block and allow for airflow between spaces.

Large program volumes like the gymnasium and performance theatre are located to the north opposite the two storey classroom block. ABOVE Glazing into the gymnasium connects the space with the Canyon and allows for increased spectator viewing.

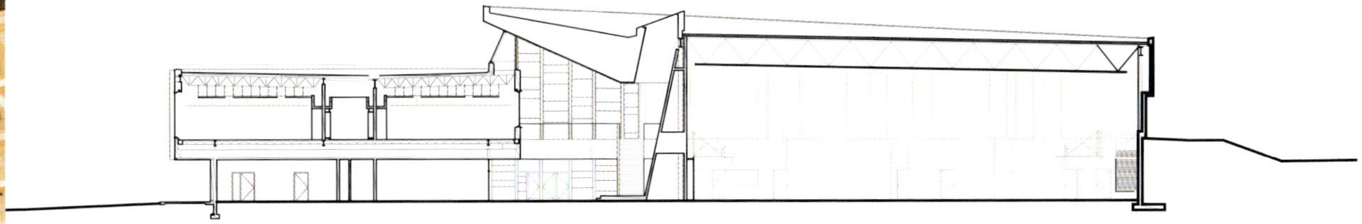

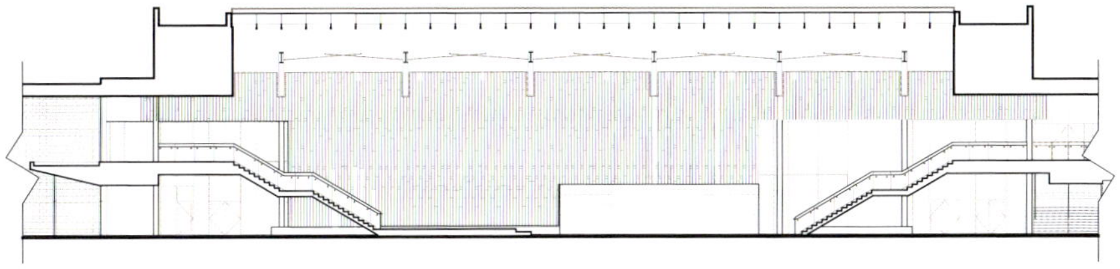

DUCHESS PARK SECONDARY

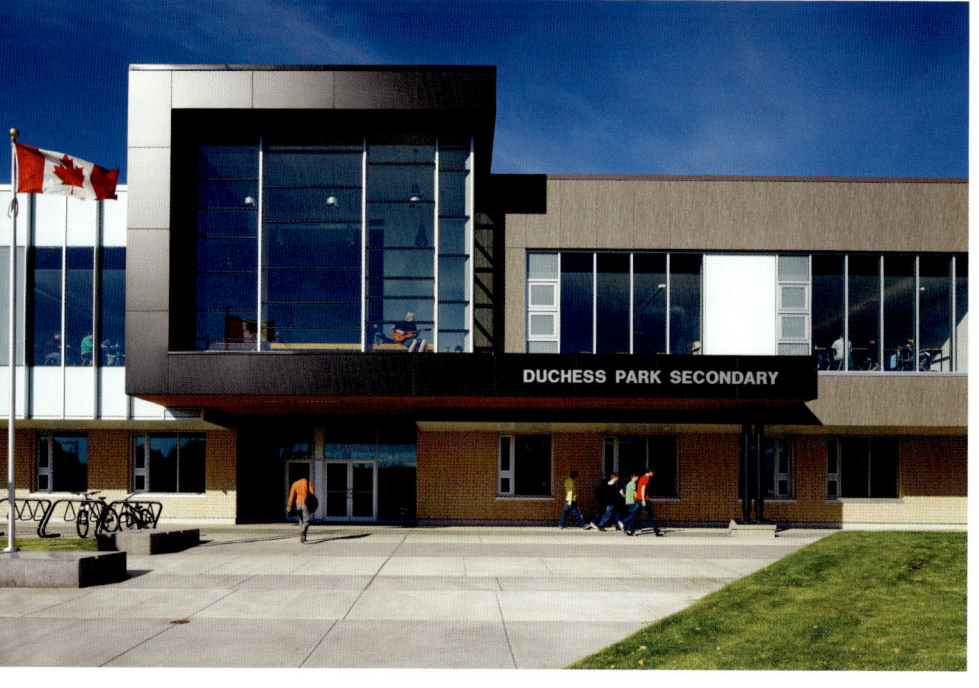

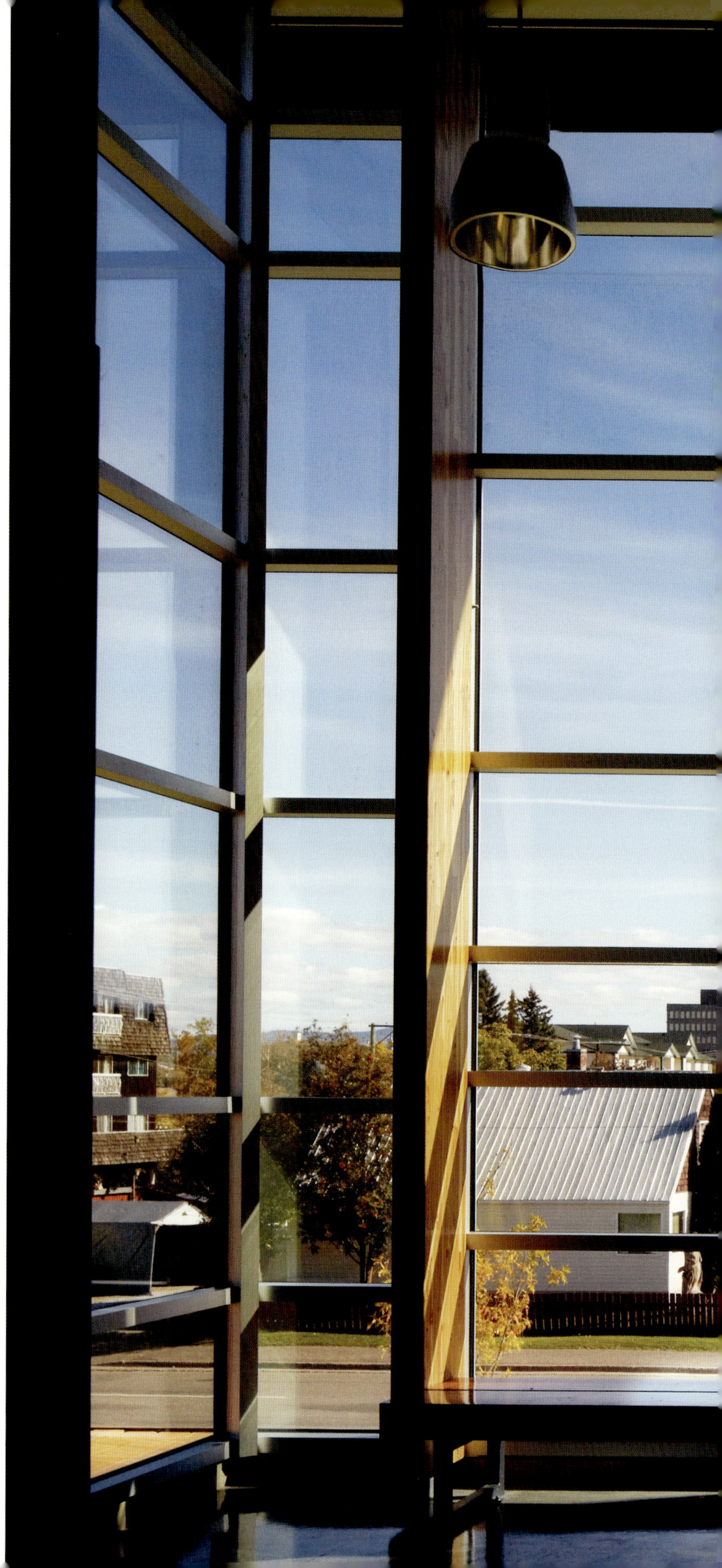

STEVESTON FIREHALL

Steveston Firehall
Richmond, BC

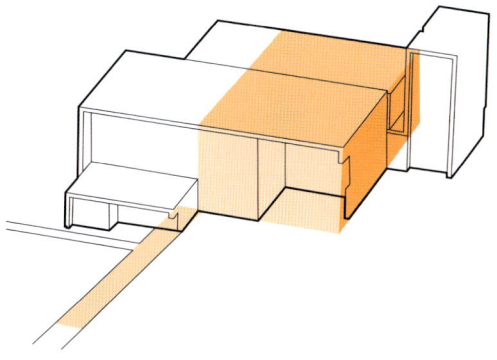

Client
City of Richmond

Year
2011

Size
840 m^2

Certification
Targeting LEED Gold Certification

Awards
2014 City of Richmond Lulu Award for Urban Design
2012 & 2014 Canadian Wood WORKS! Awards

The role of our emergency services is critical to the health, safety, and resilience of our communities. Emergency services personnel are public servants in the truest sense of the term, yet their presence is not always apparent on a daily basis. This project reflects HCMA's belief that civic infrastructure projects should create community landmarks that contribute positively to a community's identity.

After extensive study, the City of Richmond decided to replace an aging fire hall which no longer met the needs of the community, with a new post-disaster facility. Strategically located at the intersection of two arterial roads, the existing site offered the opportunity to create an iconic structure that would mark the entrance to this historic community.

The physical constraints of the site, the requirement for the existing facility to remain operational during construction, and the large turning radius of the fire trucks together determined the placement and oblique orientation of the new building.

The hose drying tower was positioned closest to the street intersection to give the building maximum visibility as a gateway to the community. Facing the street, the transparent apparatus bays, gear rooms and workshops proudly put their inner workings on public display. The administrative areas, day room, and kitchen/dining room are located away from the street for privacy and to provide quieter sleeping quarters.

The gender neutral dormitory and washrooms are located on the second floor together with a fitness area overlooking the apparatus bays. Spaces were planned to provide maximum visual and physical connection to each other and to streamline the route to the apparatus bays for minimum response times.

Fire halls include certain program elements whose form and dimensions are dictated by strict functional requirements: a hose drying tower whose height is half that of the longest hose, and apparatus bays that accommodate the largest ladder trucks. Conventional fire hall design typically relies on visually distinct forms for the apparatus bays and working and living areas. By contrast, this project employs a strategy whereby the programmatic elements are united horizontally, cross-cutting the various programmatic elements, into a cohesive whole.

The wood and metal composite building skin is folded into three distinct forms, each element folding in response to the different requirements of the program. The open ends are infilled with glass curtain walls to bring in daylight and to accommodate natural ventilation. The gaps between the folded skins become light-filled spaces, often used for circulation. Additional skylights and windows are created by cut-outs that bring natural daylight into parts of the building that would traditionally be enclosed.

BELOW These models show the exploration of the folded bands concept. The height of the building is primarily governed by the operational requirements of the apparatus bays and the training/hose tower. Three folded building skins with different heights respond to the spaces they enclose.

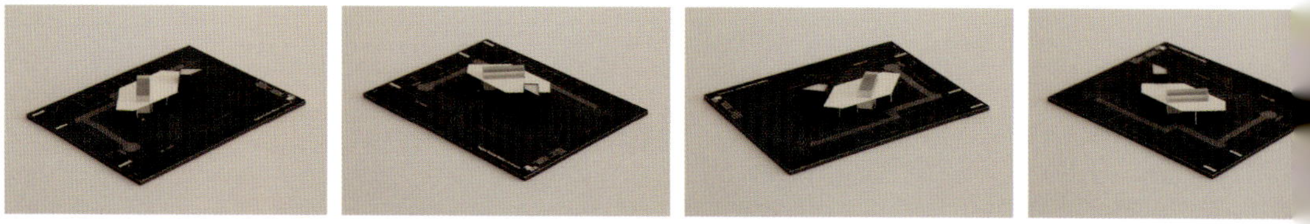

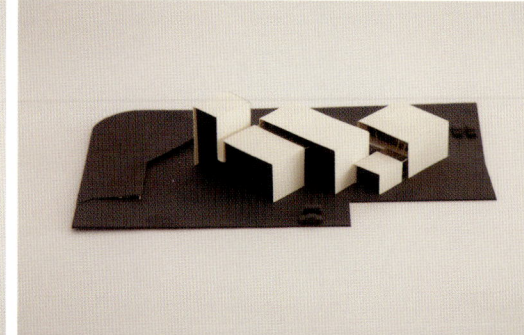

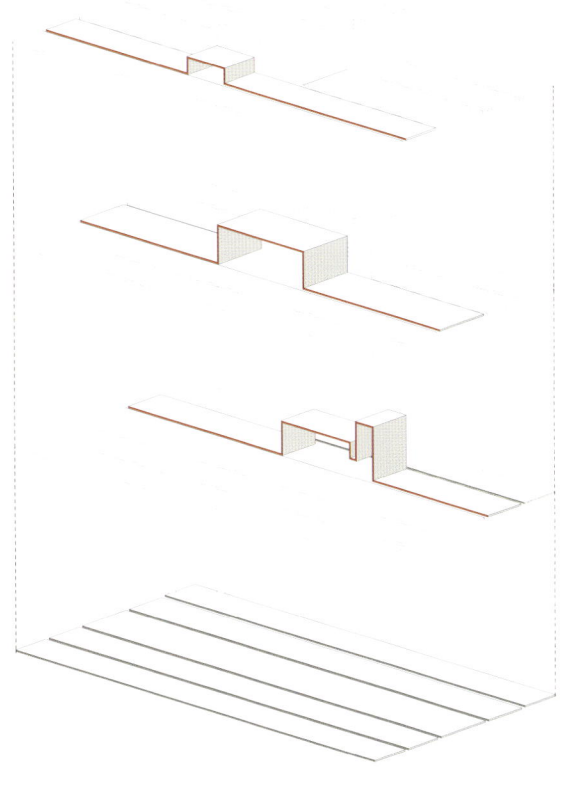

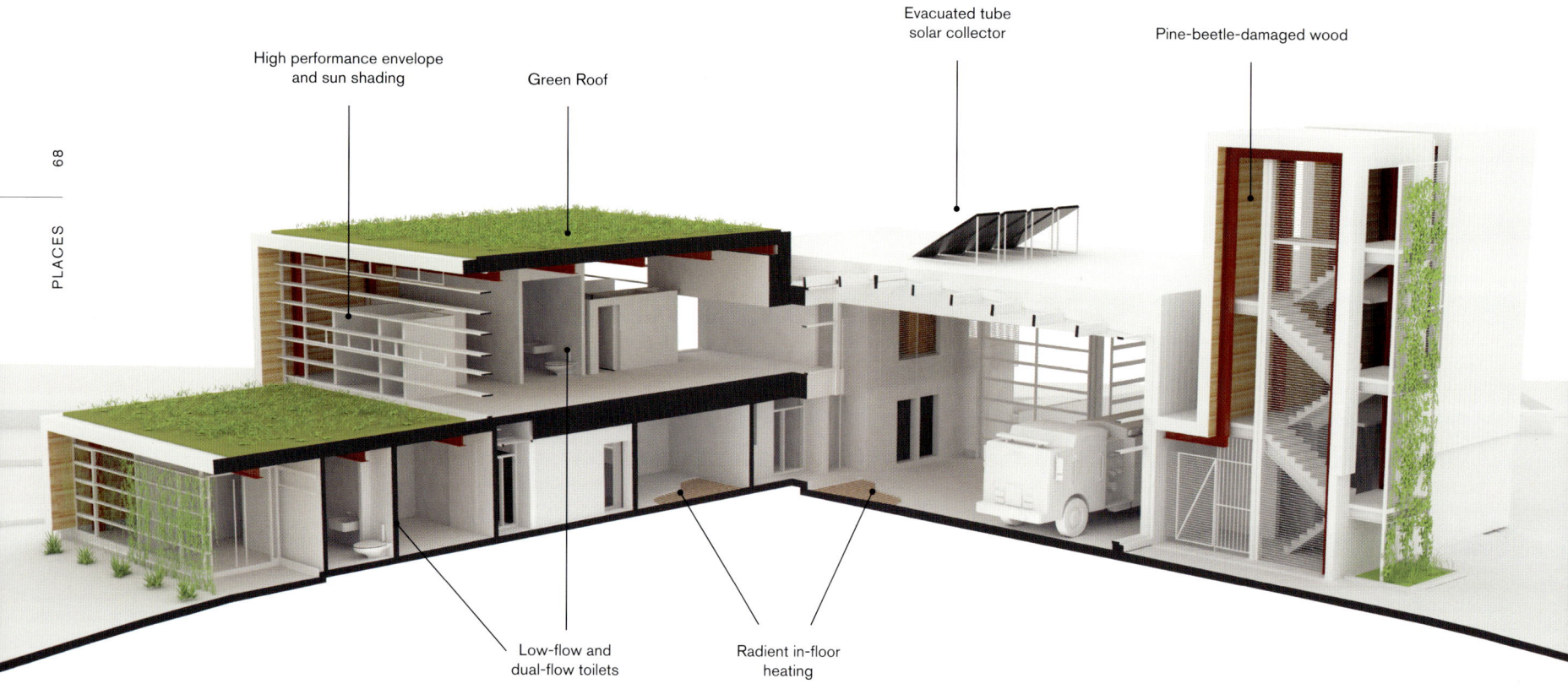

The Fire Hall was designed targeting LEED® Gold certification. The implemented sustainable strategies for this project include geothermal systems, solar water pre-heating, daylight harvesting, a green roof/wall, and rain gardens.

1 Entry
2 Vestibule
3 Training Room
4 Pre-planning Office
5 Day Room
6 Washroom
7 Captains' Office/Dorm
8 Storage
9 Janitor
10 Kitchen
11 Turn-out Gear Room
12 Communication Centre
13 Work Shop
14 Mechanical
15 Apparatus Bay
16 Hose Repair
17 Training Hose Tower

BELOW The southern public face of the building acts as the interface between private firehall operations and the public street. Fire personnel conduct some of their work in this public drive-through zone creating a transparency that supports a meaningful presence in their community.

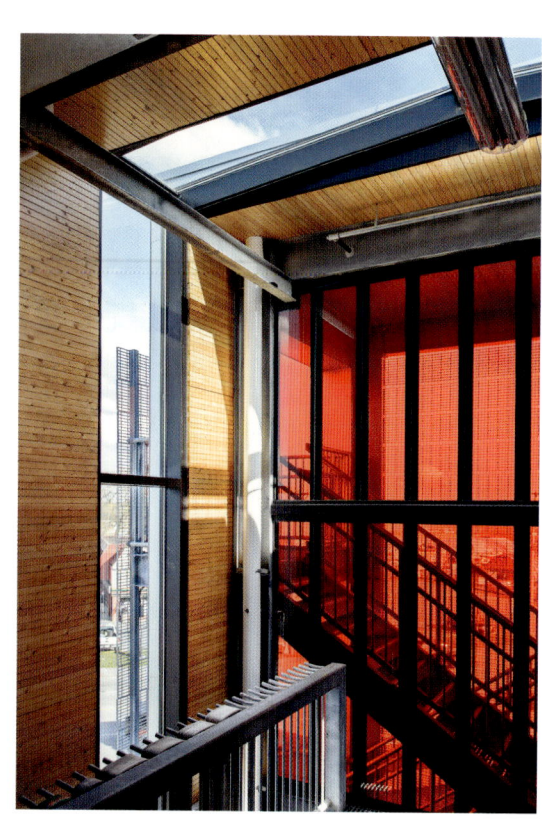
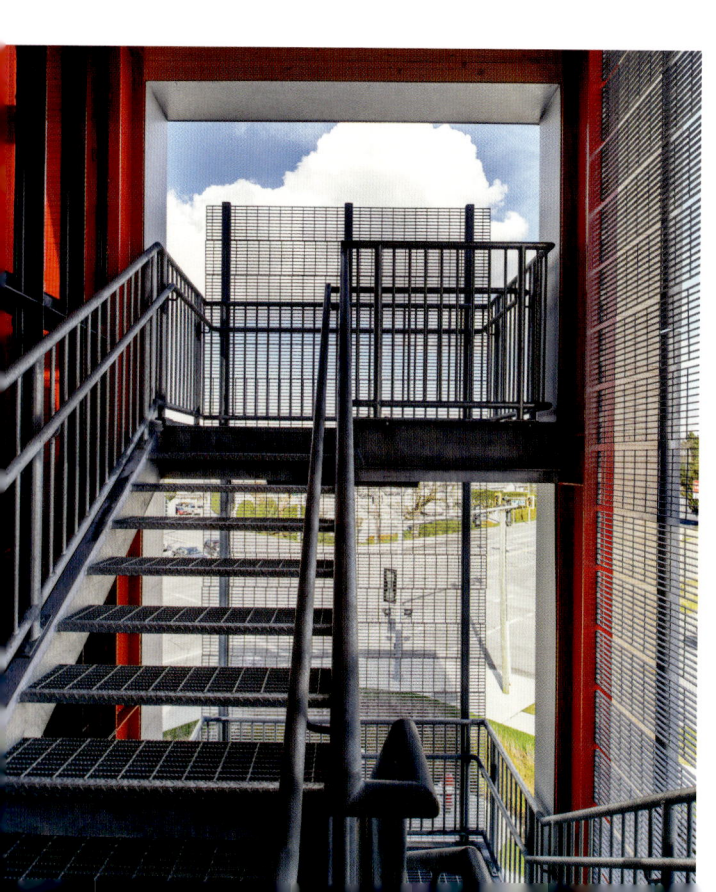

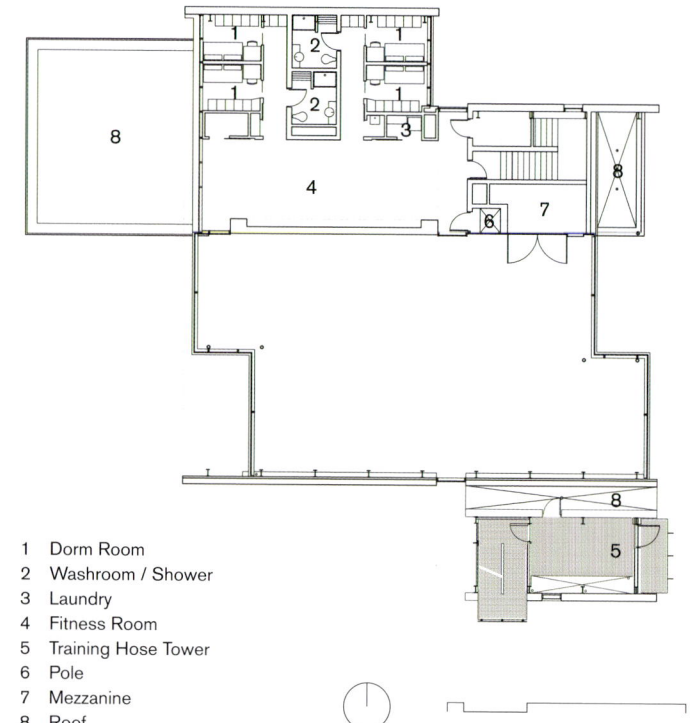

1 Dorm Room
2 Washroom / Shower
3 Laundry
4 Fitness Room
5 Training Hose Tower
6 Pole
7 Mezzanine
8 Roof

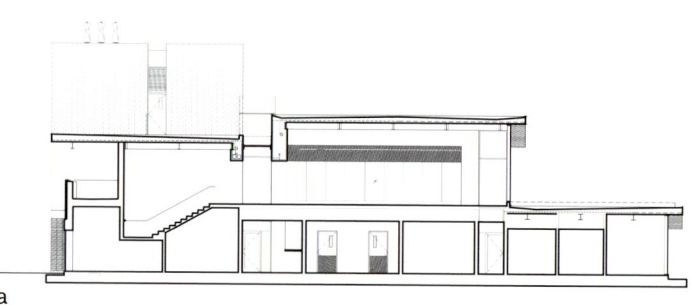

a

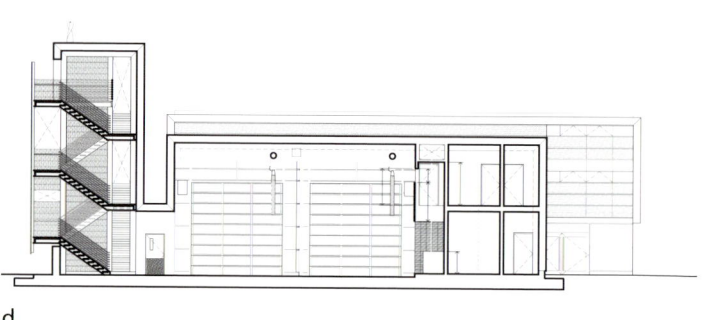

d

HCMA CULTURE

In all of their projects, HCMA strives to create an architecture of engagement—buildings that are inclusive, democratic, and which support interaction between diverse members of the community. Believing that this interaction, which is designed to empower multiple voices, is a key component of social sustainability, the office has implemented opportunities to nurture this culture internally.

One of the resulting initiatives is HCMA Days, a topical day of non-client based exploration in which the entire staff of both the Vancouver and Victoria offices are free to test, question, and create. The initiative provides an opportunity for everyone, job descriptions aside, to explore ideas without the constraints of routine project and office operations.

Each HCMA Day arises organically and is organized by a different individual or team who have taken particular interest in a current topic or process of exploration. The theme is set in advance and introduced leading up to the day so that staff can self-organize and begin in earnest in the morning. The day is punctuated by informal reviews with the final presentations taking place in the late afternoon, often the office welcomes special guests or experts on the topic.

The theme for each HCMA Day is different, and deliberately chosen to complement day to day work and allow for engagement with a current event or contemporary topic. Examples include proposals for the City of Edmonton park pavilion competition in 2010, an IDEO inspired "Day of Making" focused on prototyping in full scale, and an intervention to densify a typical single family residential block in Vancouver given the City of Vancouver's "Greenest City Action Plan."

This latter project, designed to draw attention to the necessity of change, but to offer solutions that were innovative and inspiring, drew responses at a variety of scales: from a redesigned mailbox to a suspended megacity, whose supporting legs touched down between the existing houses.

The most recent exercise in 2013, inspired by an initiative led by Scot Hein at the City of Vancouver, was a cultural mapping of public spaces that were of personal significance to each individual in the office. The idea was to expand the understanding of the city from that of a physical construct to one that included the social and cultural dimensions of place. Again, the responses were diverse—from bustling sidewalk cafes, to secluded rocks in the forest. The success of this exercise led to its being repeated in the Social Sustainability course HCMA taught at UBC School of Architecture and Landscape Architecture (SALA) in the winter 2014 semester.

HCMA Day has been successful in creating continuity between internal community dynamics and the philosophy that guides their design projects for clients. The office believes that the social benefits that are realized internally in terms of team building and collaboration can be carried beyond the office, extending into the communities in which individual staff members live.

Dencity Day / 2012

Introduction

We are asking you to grapple with the question of density on the typical single family lot in Vancouver. Are current levels of density sustainable? Do they need to change in order to support new demands for living on the perimeter of Vancouver's downtown core? You can take on as much or little as you want. Feel free to take on the grid, the block, the lot, or the front door. Interventions of any and all scales are encouraged. Be practical or be outrageous. For this exercise we are providing a generic Westside RS1 block of full size city lots. At 33' x 120' you can capitalize on zoning allowances for laneway houses or question if this is enough. You might look at the swaths of blacktop that are used to move and store automobiles or the acres of lawns that form empty front yards.

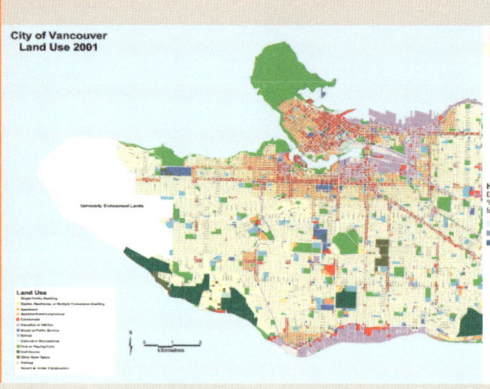
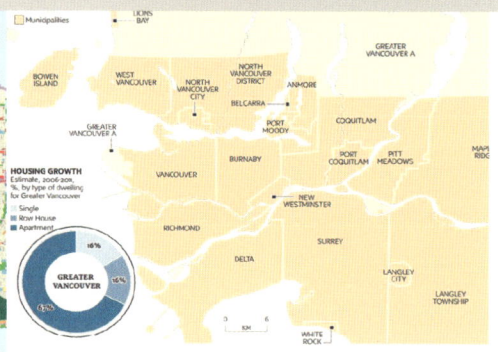
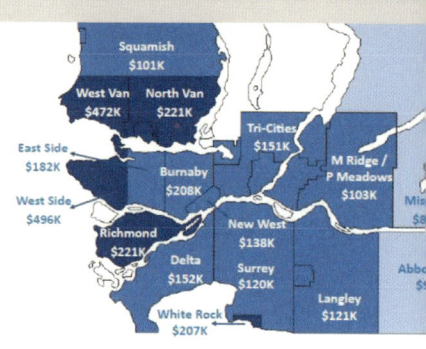

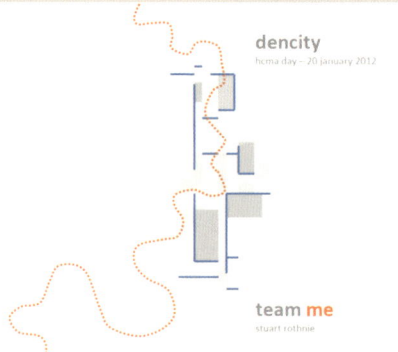

team me
stuart rothnie

dencity — community — a thread that binds us

context — context

Team GK
Gregory L. Knight

NO MAN IS RICH ENOUGH TO BUY BACK HIS PAST
— Oscar Wilde

AND THEN EVERYONE LIVED HAPPILY EVER AFTER
Goldilocks.. Or someone

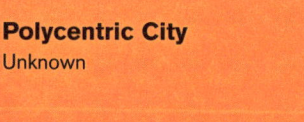

Polycentric City
Unknown

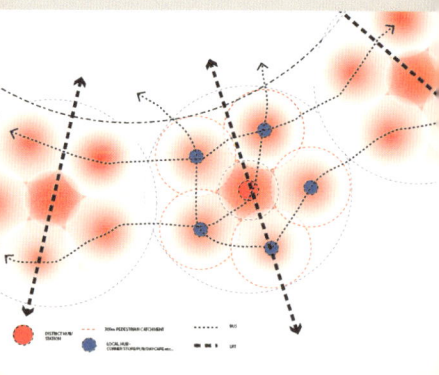

City of Vancouver Land Use			
Type	Acres	Km Sq	%
Single Family	9,308	37.67	32%
Multi Family	2,503	10.13	9%
Duplex, Rowhouse	828	3.35	3%
Apartment	1,386	5.61	5%
Mixed Apartment & Commercial	289	1.17	1%
Streets, Lanes, Sidewalks	8,332	33.72	29%

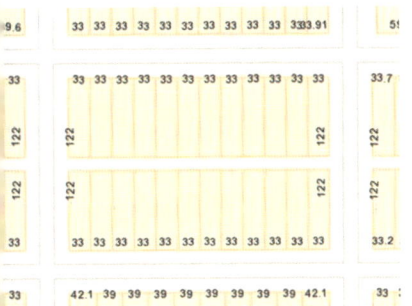

Team Me
Stuart Rothnie

Insertions The Premise... Keep the established grain and insert forms within the gaps. Like pouring grout between the tiles, new smaller scale insertions can blend and join neighbourhoods without wholesale change. To do this means eroding the current setbacks and blurring the legal lot lines to create other opportunities and mix. The keys are to create more interaction and social mixing by providing local public spaces and connecting to the sidewalks and public realm. Creating nodes, connections and assembling another grain of secondary enclosing walls.

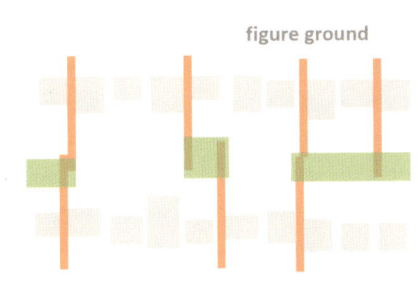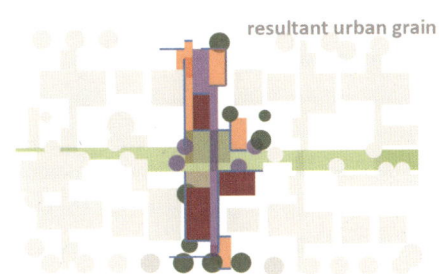

figure ground resultant urban grain

Capitalizm Unleashed
Team Max Power

TEAM MAX POWER PRESENTS
"CAPITALISM UNLEASHED"

Light Making / 2013

The day will be an exercise of making a shade or shades for a light source, and it can be built from any material you choose. The day will start out with a short presentation, explaining the process and steps for the day, and then each person will be building models prototypes and more finished product (s). We have Victor Quezada and Sean Casey, Principals of Render Planning + Lighting, attending in the afternoon as our guests.

They will be bringing a range of lamp types / sources to test out your creations. This is a day of making…no computers allowed. No group work…this day is about participation…For this event we need materials…over the next few days can you bring into the office any small materials of any kind that might be used for this exercise…cardboard, fabric, card, paper, Styrofoam, wood scraps, felt, plastic etc… whatever inspires you.

Lindsay Csabak | Aiden Callison | Stephanie McWilliams

Adam Fawkes | Melissa Higgs | Philip Stolton | Dara Wone | Carl-Jan Rupp | Derek Wong

Kirsten Meissner | Paul Rigby | Jay Lin | Rance Mok

say Csabak Elise Woestyn Patrick Wheeler Michael Henderson

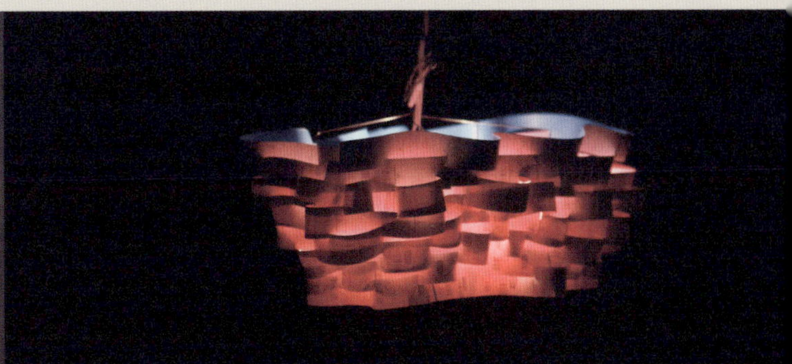

Elena Chernyshov

Darryl Johnson 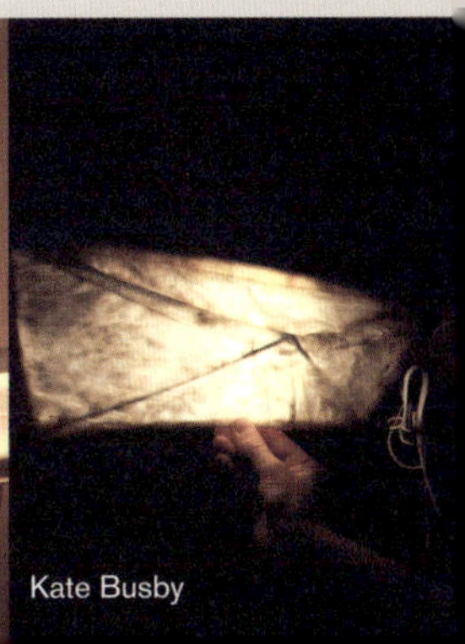 Kate Busby

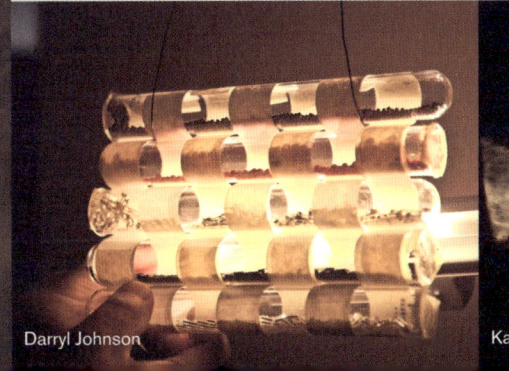

Social Sustainability / 2014

The focus of our next Day of Making will be to explore the topic of social sustainability*, and in particular the role and special/significant/unique/"gifted" urban spaces play in developing and building a socially sustainable city. Your advance assignment for next Friday is:

Choose an urban space in the public realm (anywhere, any place) that you have connected with on a personal level. Ideally this will be a space that you consider to be a significant contributor to community building and social sustainability. The focus of the day will be to explore the significant aspects of that space/place. Come prepared with materials that you can use during the day to create a presentation of your place to the rest of us. The presentation can take any form – collage, sketches, video, poetry. More details to follow next Friday...

*Social sustainability is the least defined and least understood of the three pillar of sustainability and sustainable development. The triad of Environmental Sustainability, Economic Sustainability, and Social Sustainability is widely accepted as a model for addressing sustainability, yet the social aspect has had considerably less attention in public dialogue. The concept of Social Sustainability encompasses such topics as: responsibility, social justice, cultural competence, community resilience, and human adaptation. - Wikipedia

Miroir Eau, Bordeaux, FR
Elise Woestyn

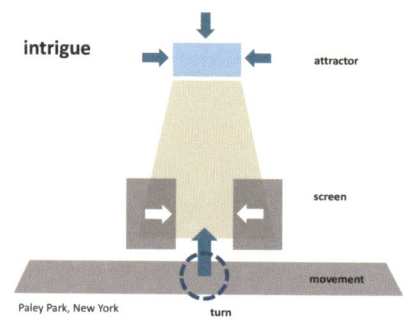
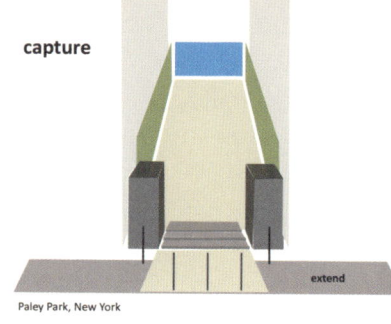

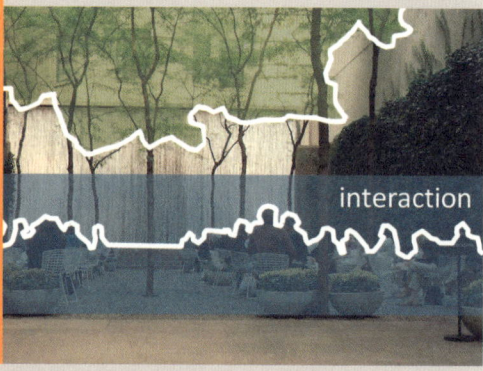
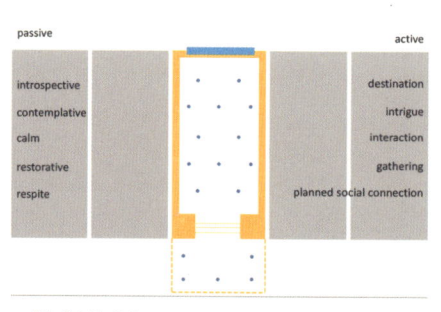

Maple Square, Vancouver
Steve DiPasquale

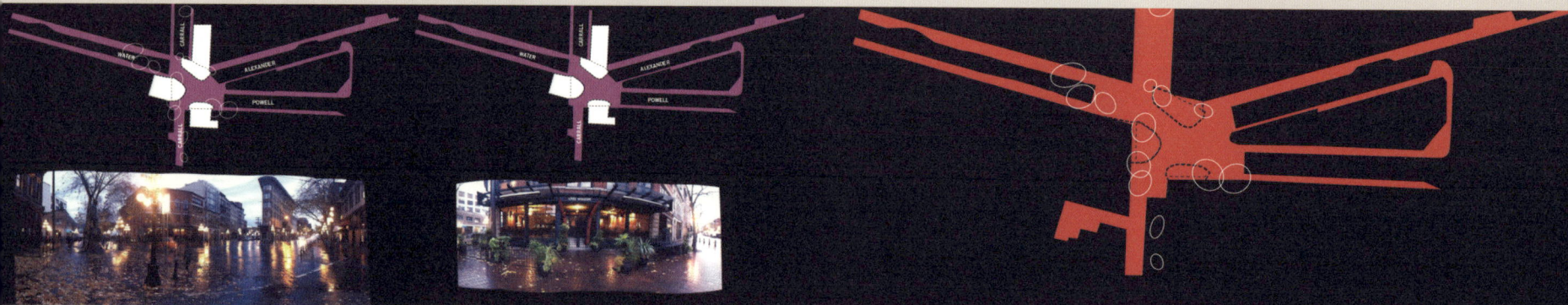

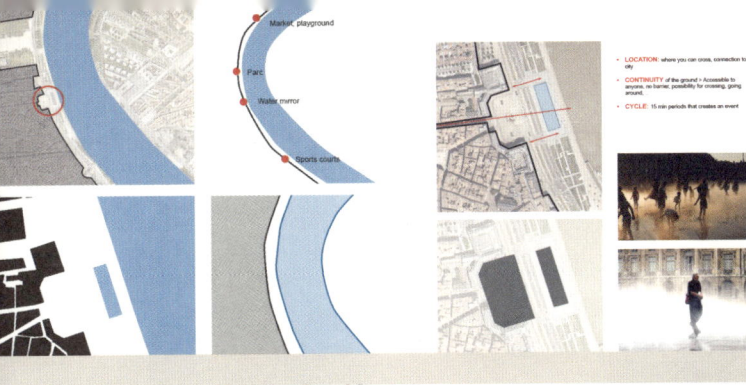

Paley Park, NY
Stuart Rothnie

Paley Park, New York

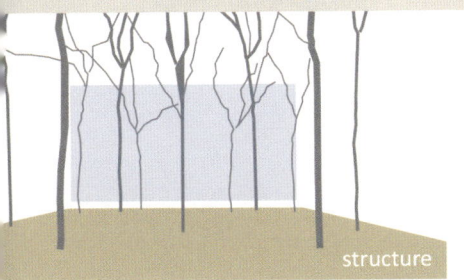

structure

Paley Park, New York

canopy "ceiling"

Paley Park, New York

flux

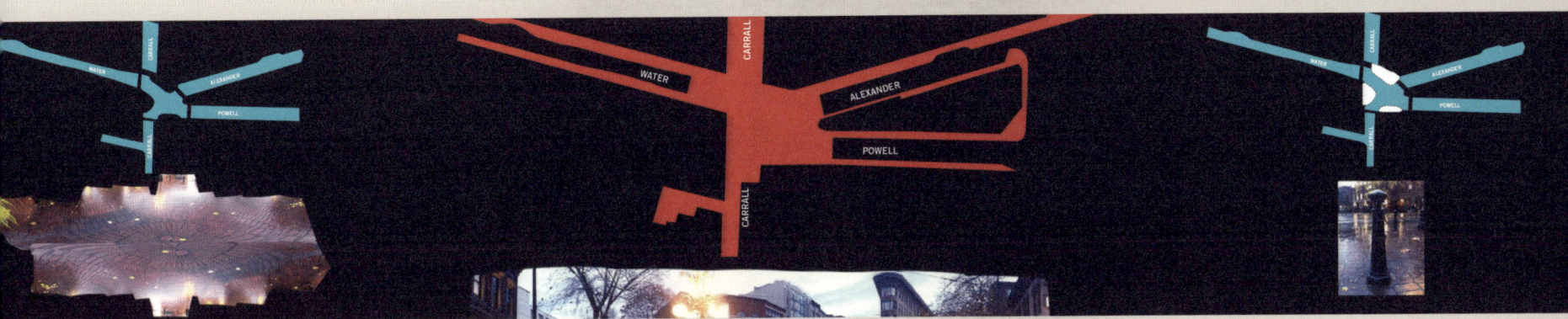

Hinge Park
Melissa Higgs

Hinge Park

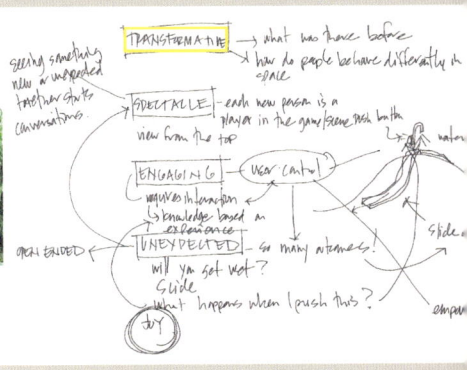

TRANSFORMATION
↳ PLACE MAKING
↓
ENGAGING + UNEXPECTED + SPECTACLE
↓
JOY

Defining the Edge
Paul Fast

DEFINING THE EDGE

SHELTER
OPPORTUNITY
REST
INSTINCT
SAFETY

DEFINING THE EDGE

AIR and Faraday Cafe

The HCMA Architecture + Design Artist-In-Residence (AIR) program was developed by the company in 2014 as part of a broad strategy to examine the potential of the practice's work to contribute to social sustainability goals. This initiative continues the research started by Darryl Condon (Managing Principal at HCMA) who offered a course in Social Sustainability to students of UBC's School of Architecture and Landscape Architecture. HCMA | AIR is meant to stimulate discussion and challenge preconceptions about the limits of architectural practice. The program invites artists to investigate the interface between the public realm and people through an exploration of the boundaries between architecture and the artist's creative field.

Artists working in a variety of media are encouraged to participate, including visual arts, video, photography, theatre and writing. Throughout the course of the residency, artists collaborate with the staff at HCMA, discussing issues related to their work and to the project, and exploring themes related to social sustainability. Resident artists have access to the resources of the office (including computers, plotters, printers and model shop) and are supported with an honorarium and materials budget.

The first installment of this exciting new program was an installation piece titled "Faraday Café" by social artist Julien Thomas. From July 2 to 16, Julien and HCMA invited the public to experience the only coffee shop that actually repels wireless signals. A simple question generated the project: In a space devoid of cell phone or data connections, will personal connection be formed instead? To accomplish this, a room was constructed around a picnic table and then that room was enclosed entirely in an aluminum mesh that shields electromagnetic signals. Throughout the installation, the artist served a rotation of artisanal coffees and teas to curious customers, and hosted a series of events including meditation sessions, afternoon DJ sets, storytelling gatherings and potluck dinners.

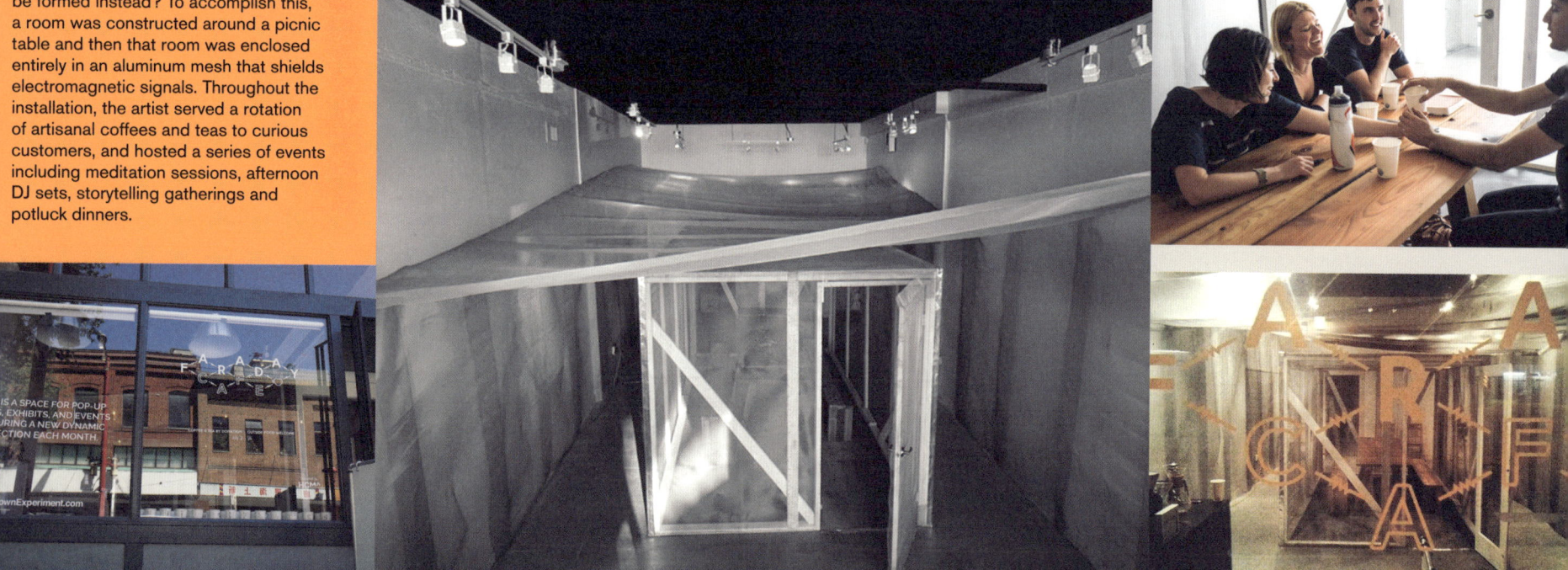

WITHOUT THE INTERNET,
I think better.

WITHOUT THE INTERNET,
I felt a bit naked, but the good kind of naked. :)

We talked. And didn't look at the score.

WITHOUT THE INTERNET,
MY PHONE STILL DOES A WHOLE LOT.

ARETHA'S GOLD

FARADAY
CAFE
COFFEE & TEA BY DONATION
OUTSIDE FOOD WELCOME

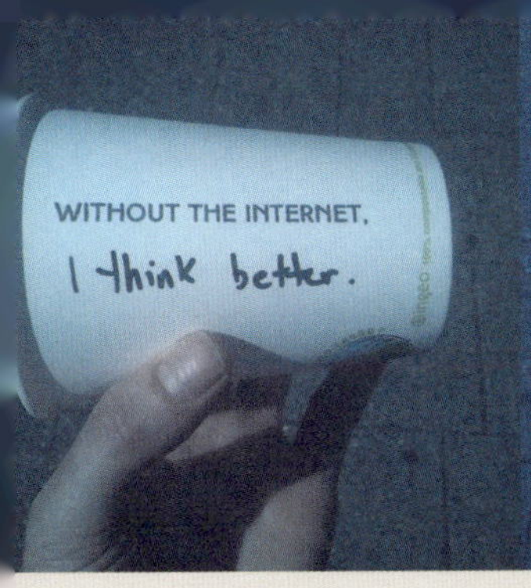

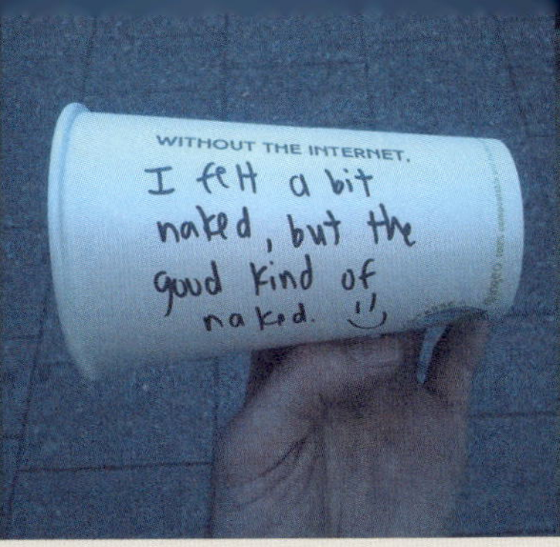

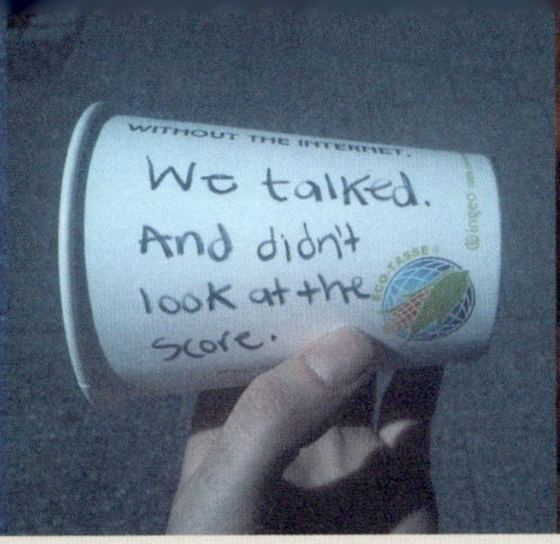

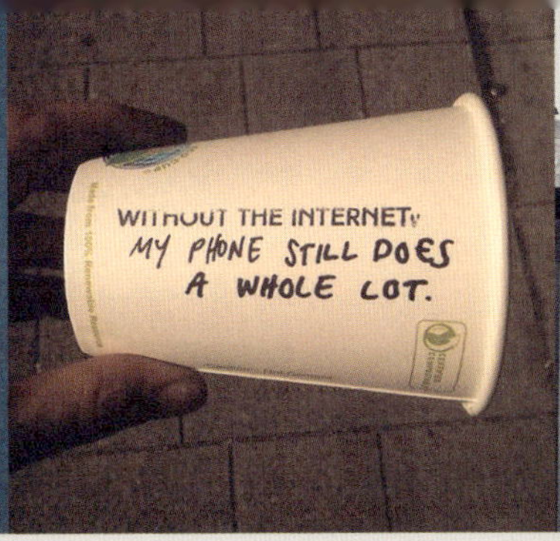

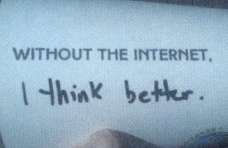

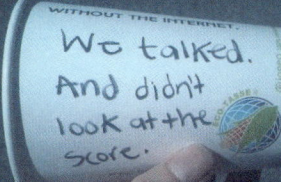

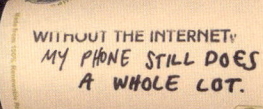

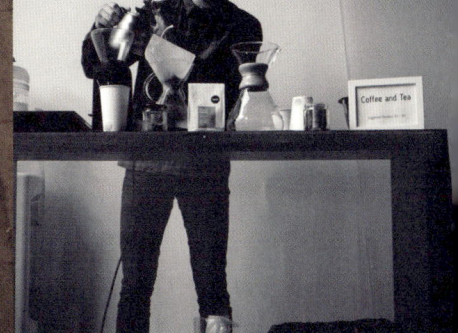

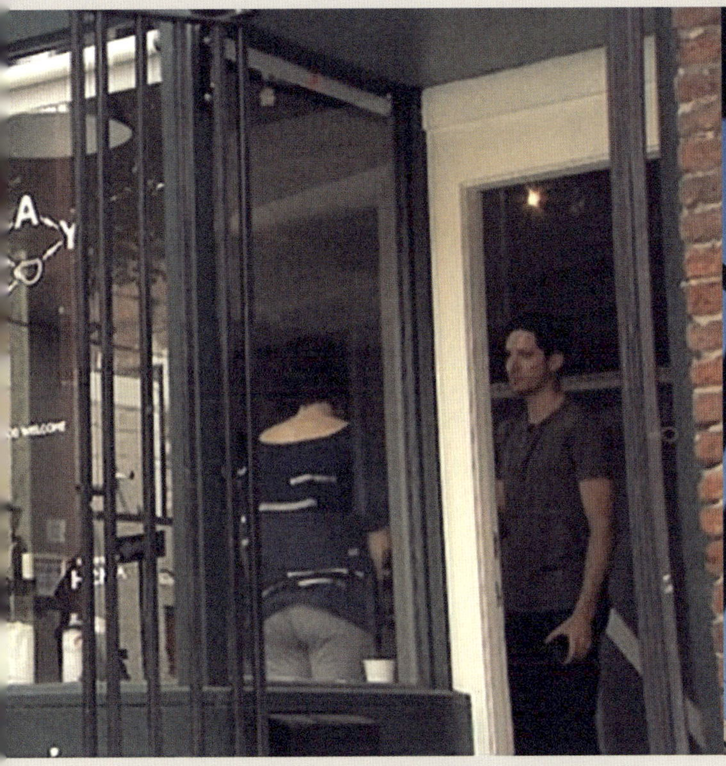

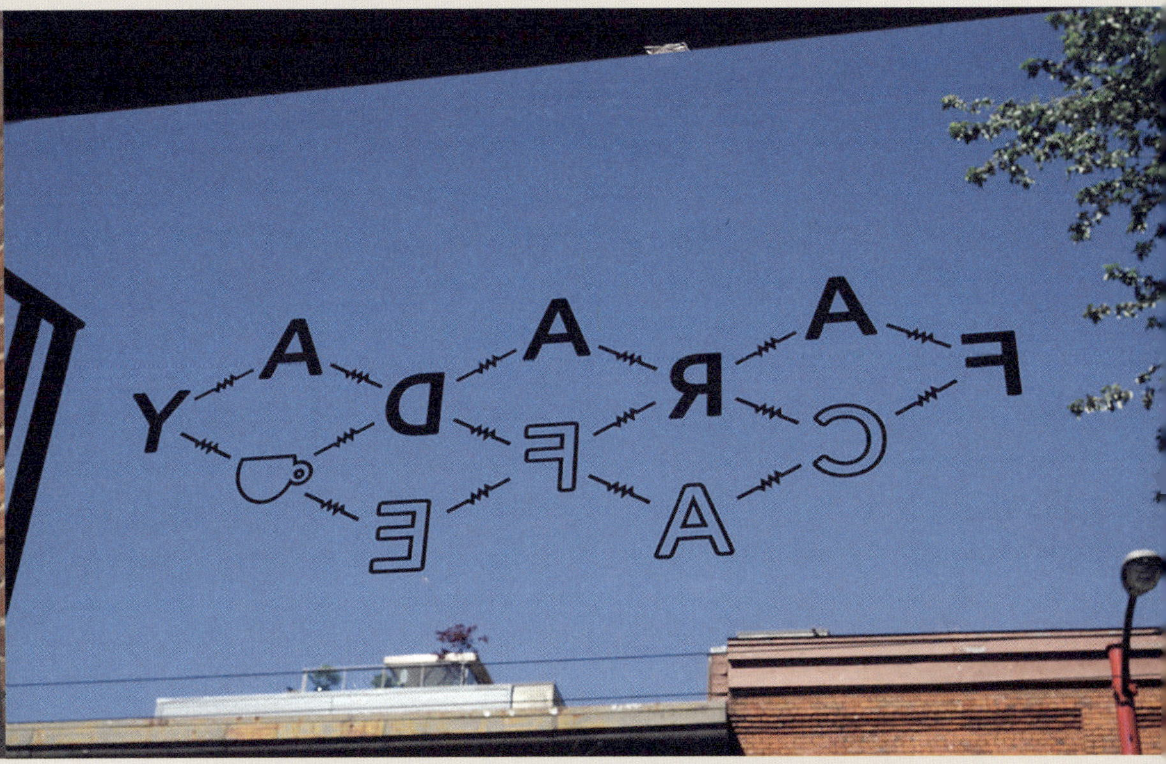

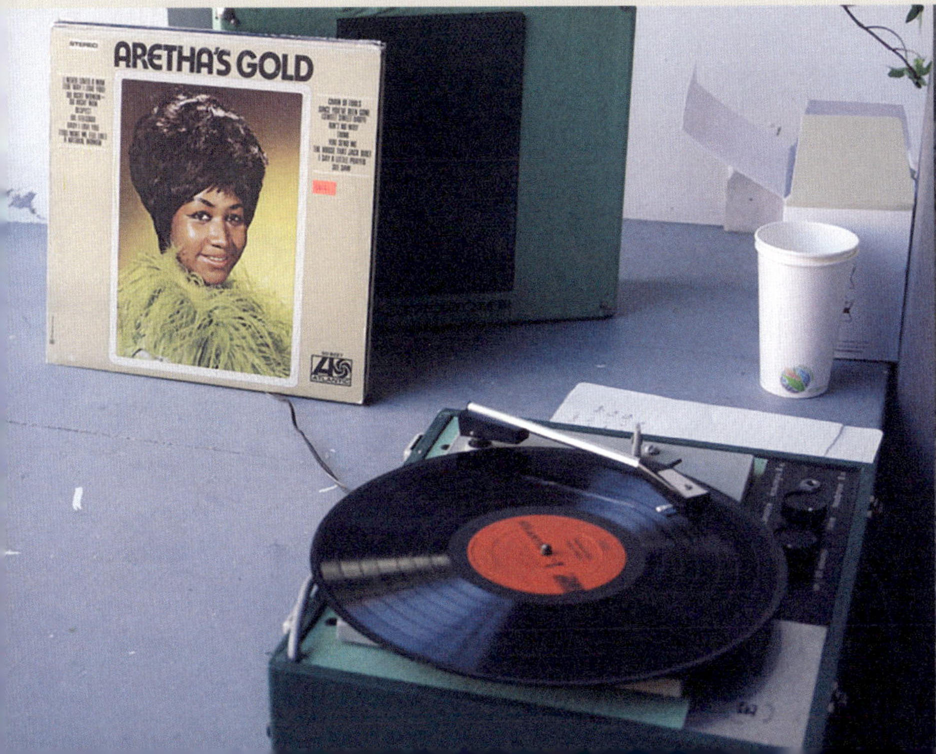

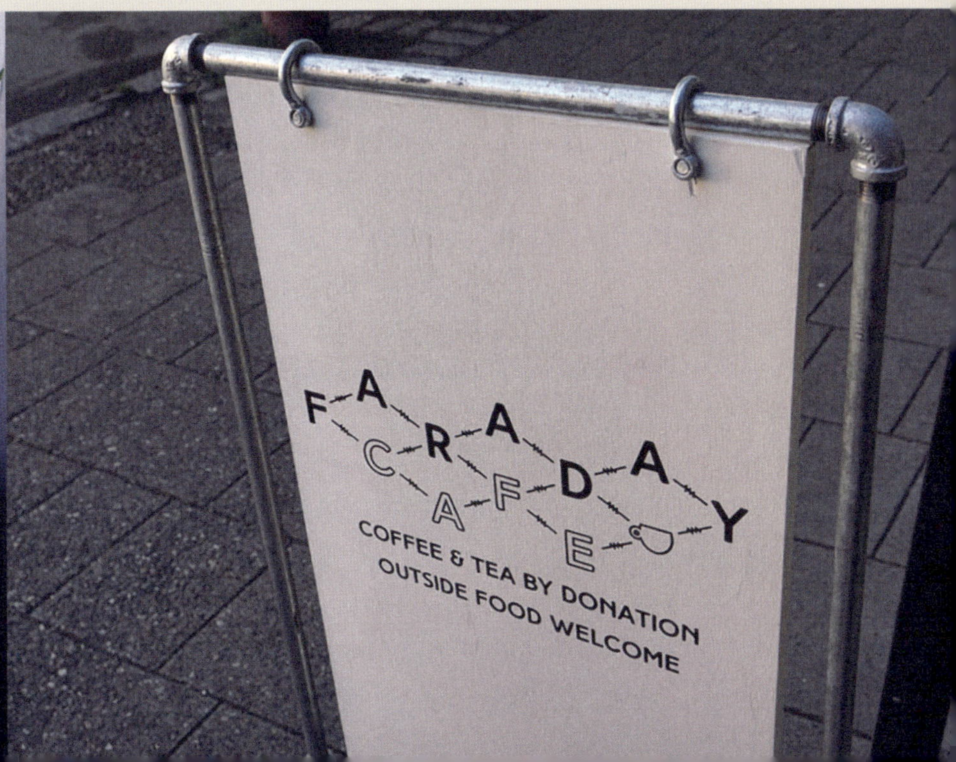

Building Blocks Playhouse
Canfor Playhouse Challenge Entry 2012, Vancouver, BC

Canfor Forest Products Ltd. launched its Playhouse Challenge in 2012, with all seven entries in the inaugural competition being erected at the annual Pacific National Exhibition in Vancouver. Each playhouse is a collaborative project with a BC forest products company donating building materials, an architectural team contributing their creativity in design, and a local builder providing their expertise in construction.

The concept for the project, dubbed "Building Blocks House," is based on an observation that children find delight in simple things (like a box), often more so than the extravagant toys that arrive in the box itself. Beyond a fascination with something as simple as a cardboard box, children also love to explore.

The playhouse consists of two interlocking volumes, one finished in bright red and one left as natural wood. Each is comprised of a series of spaces of varying scale and size. Built on a 2'x2' module from marine grade plywood and simple cedar furring strips, the playhouse allows for endless variations of a journey through a series of twisting, interconnected spaces.

The Building Blocks Playhouse was the result of an in-house design competition (a common practice at HCMA that fosters a creative culture in the office) at HCMA; and the winning design was then further developed to the detailed design level. The playhouse was of necessity a "placeless" object (as its final location was unknown) and had no requirement for a weatherproof envelope. This permitted the design to focus on the exploration and articulation of space at the scale of the child.

It also presented the opportunity to collaborate with other professionals in a different and less constrained context. In this sense, the act of creation anticipated the acts of play that the completed structure would encourage—a departure point for the imagination, rather than a pre-ordained response.

The playhouse elicits a wide range of responses from those who encounter it. This reveals the shortcomings of our contemporary culture of space, play, and imagination in which a formulaic approach to the design of playground equipment limits the opportunities for creative play. After being explored and experienced by thousands of children at the PNE, the Building Blocks Playhouse was voted the most popular of the seven entries and received the People's Choice Award.

Following the Exhibition, the playhouses were auctioned off, with the proceeds going to a number of Habitat for Humanity affordable housing projects throughout British Columbia; the structures themselves were gifted to various charities. Finning Canada purchased the Building Blocks Playhouse, who subsequently donated it to the Kootenay Child Development Centre in Cranbrook.

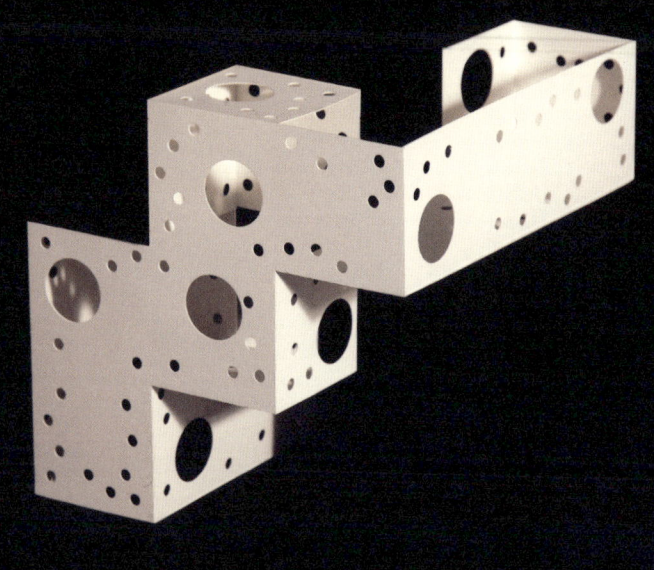

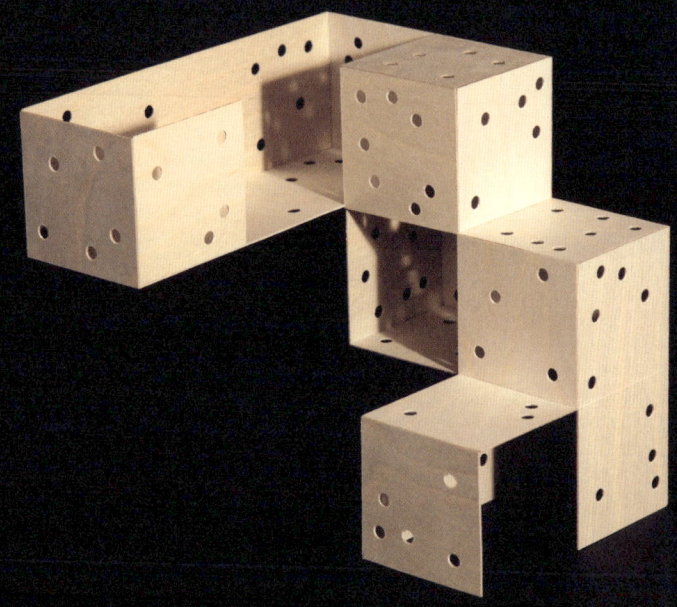

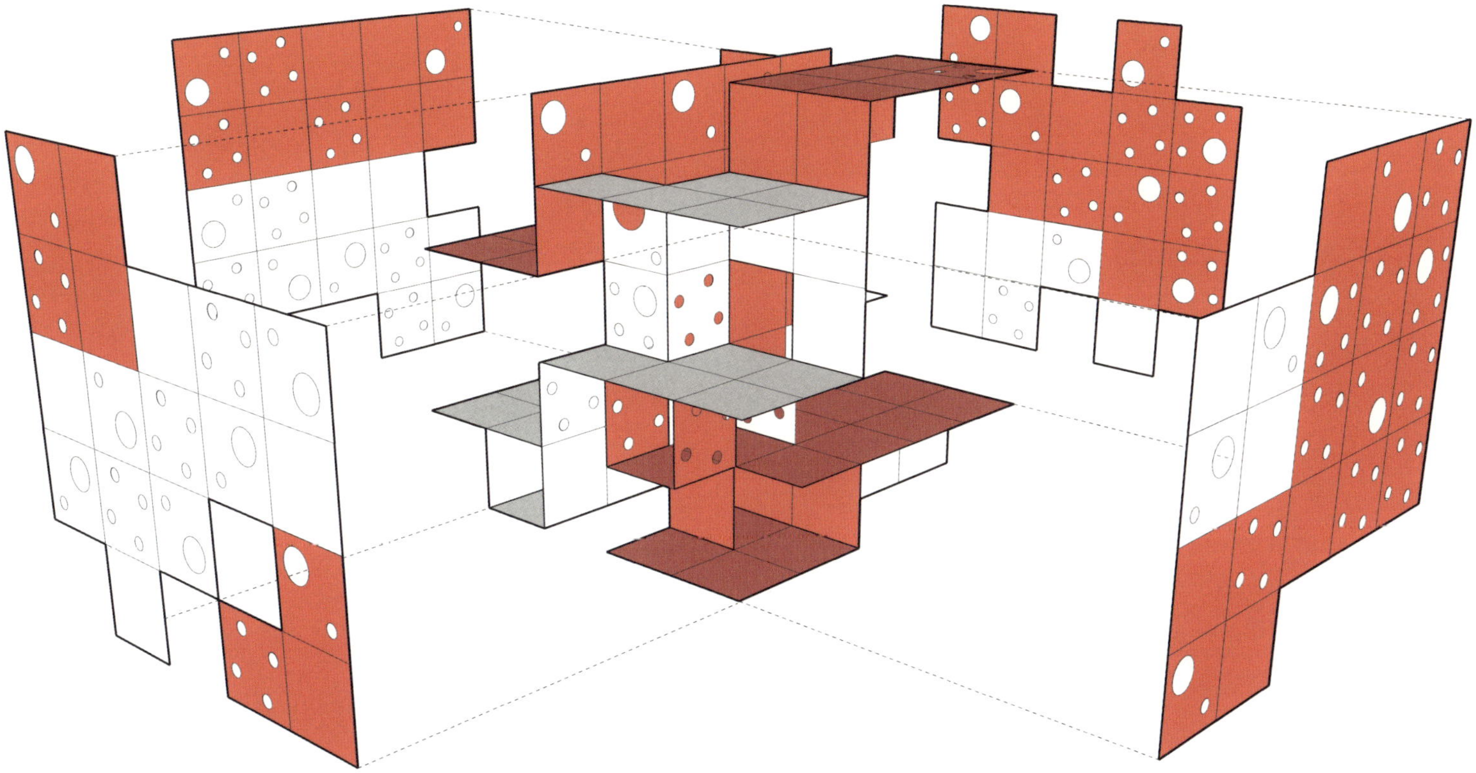

ABOVE The concept of the Building Blocks Playhouse is based on the observation that children find delight in simple things like boxes; often times the boxes toys come packaged in are enjoyed more than the toys themselves.

ABOVE Through the repetition of simple box forms an interior complexity is created encouraging exploration and play.

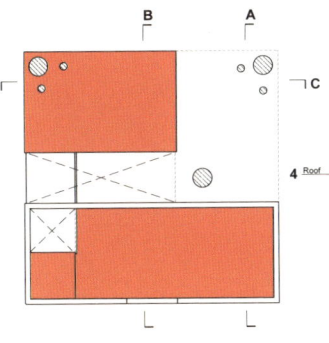
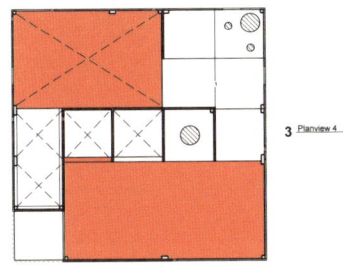
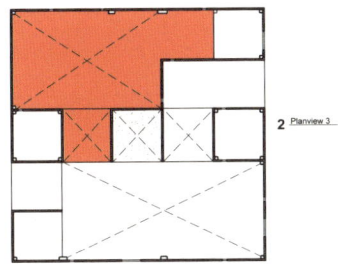
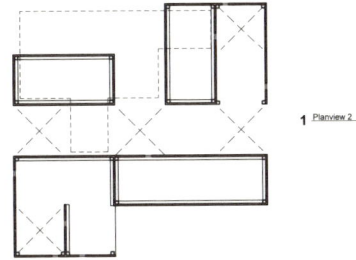
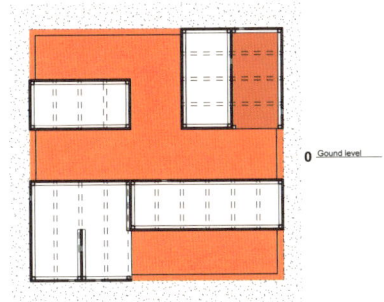

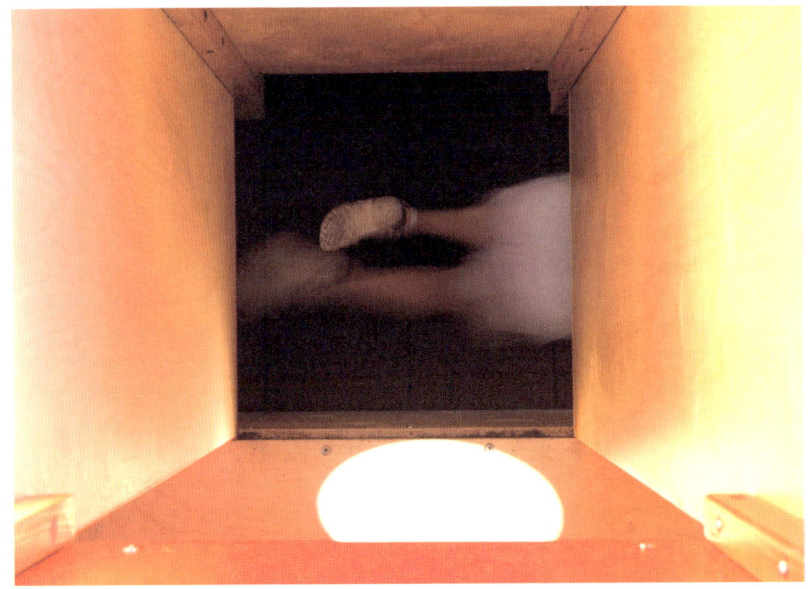

LEFT Schematic floor plans reveal the interlocking of white and red volumes.

Wall House
Canfor Playhouse Challenge Entry 2014, Vancouver, BC

HCMA participated in the Playhouse Challenge for a second time in 2014. This time, only the winning playhouse entry would be built by Canfor. HCMA's team developed three concepts and enlisted the help of some guest critics (employee's children) to help select a design.

The Wall House offers a playful take on the form and wood frame construction of the traditional house, breaking it apart into 5 walls, with play opportunities inserted into the leftover spaces. Playhouse explorers can find a new route, climb a wall, escape down a slide, or spy from a chimney. The possibilities for adventures are endless…

HCMA's entry into the Playhouse Challenge was again voted People's Choice through online votes and votes by visitors to the Pacific National Exhibition. The playhouse will be constructed in 2015.

LEFT   HCMA staff children were invited to a Friday crit session to help select the winning design for 2014 Playhouse Challenge entry.

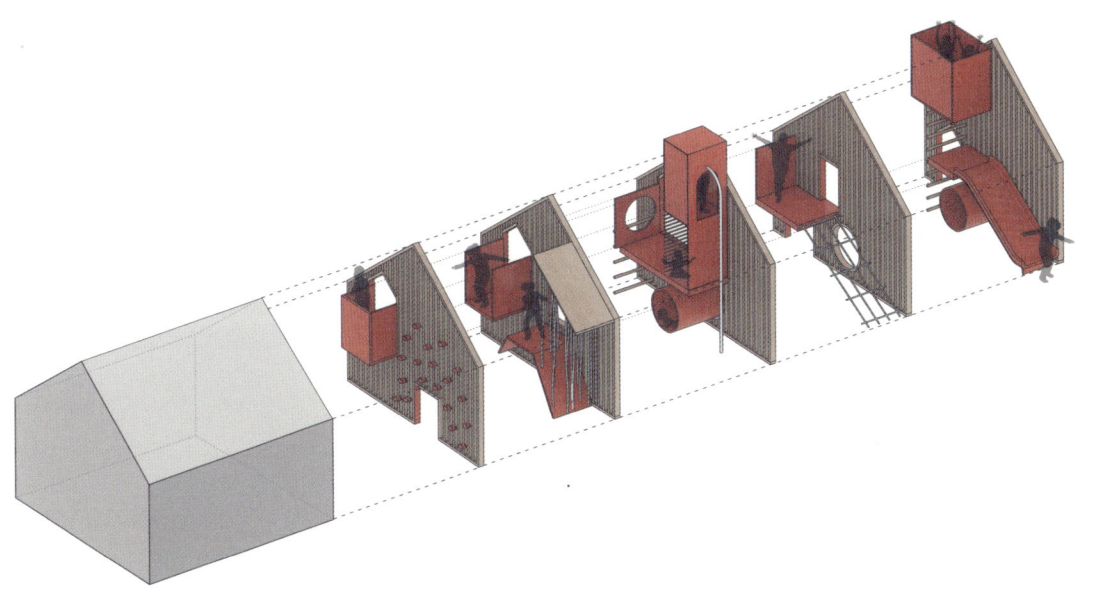

UBC SALA Course: Social Sustainability in Practice
By Melissa Higgs

…a process for creating sustainable, successful places that promote well-being, by understanding what people need from the places they live and work. Social sustainability combines the design of the physical realm with the design of the social world – infrastructure to support social and cultural life, social amenities, systems for citizen engagement and space for people and places to evolve.
—The Young Foundation

In the fall of 2013, Darryl Condon was offered the opportunity to teach a course on social sustainability at the University of British Columbia School of Architecture and Landscape Architecture (UBC SALA). Social sustainability was a concept that Condon and HCMA had been exploring and practicing for some time, and teaching the course presented the firm with an opportunity to investigate and question the topic in a more focused way, free from the constraints of day-to-day practice. The course content and development was opened for review and discussion to the entire staff—and some of the early questions we asked ourselves were:

"What is social sustainability?"

"What does it mean to our practice as Architects?"

"What aspects of social sustainability can we meaningfully impact in our work?"

These and other questions did not have immediate or easy answers, and the development of the SALA course, much like our design process, was a journey. And so, Arch573f - *Social Sustainability in Practice* was born. The course title is a reflection of what we determined the focus of the course should be: an exploration of social sustainability as it related specifically to the practice of architecture. The course was then developed into three sections: Principles (Why), Processes (How), and Products (What). Various members of HCMA staff contributed material for each section of the course, and weekly lunchtime sessions were held where readings, which had been assigned to the students for that week's course, were discussed and debated. This parallel process of discussions and investigations, both in the classroom and the studio, became an integral part of the efforts to infuse the office with the teachings of the course.

The early classes in the Principles section looked at the history of social sustainability in architecture, from the City Beautiful movement, Arts and Crafts, the rise of Modernism and the Bauhaus, Christopher Alexander's *Pattern Language* and others leading to present day. This section also led us to explore the various definitions of social sustainability and ultimately led us to adopt a working definition that we found most resonated with us most as architects which is the definition quoted above developed by the Young Foundation. Its appeal is in its clear acknowledgement of *design*—not only of the physical but also of the social realm. It also touches on some of the key principles referenced earlier in this book, and applied in our practice, like Alexandros Washburn's idea of public space being "where citizens can meet as equals, where societies build trust," and Jane Jacob's belief in the daily social interactions as the "glue" that holds a community together. This section of the course also led us to discussions about the role of social sustainability in

Student project: Alexander Ring

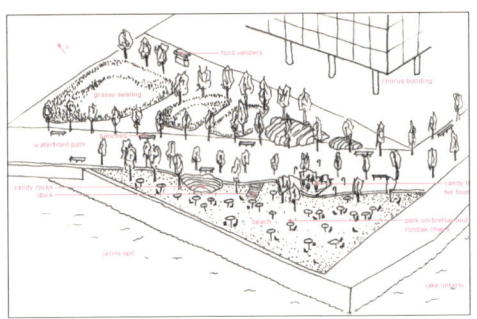

developing community resilience: what role does our connection to our neighbours—next door, on the next block, or five streets over—play in a community's ability to face future environmental and economic challenges? How does architecture in its built form influence and shape those important connections?

During the Principles section of the course we also developed a comparison of Maslow's Hierarchy of Needs pyramid, which starts at the base with Safety Needs, then moves up to Social Needs (Belonging, Acceptance), to Esteem Needs (respect for self and others) to the top of the pyramid where Self Actualization is reached. This peak of the pyramid is where Maslow believed knowledge and understanding were reached, and that human curiosity and exploration became possible. In the course, we developed our own pyramid of Social Sustainability.

The Processes and Products section of the course looked more closely at design strategies aimed at creating social sustainability outcomes, exploring the idea of "social design thinking" as it relates to HCMA's practice. Several architects, and a landscape architect practicing outside HCMA, were also invited to present their own thinking on social sustainability, and to present socially sustainable aspects of their work, which offered the students not only a wider range of viewpoints, but also a range of typologies, scales, design approach and forms of practice within which socially sustainable work was being produced locally.

The student's research investigations focused on developing community engagement strategies, a tool that will prove to be invaluable as they move forward in their development as architects.

Ultimately, our message was that buildings, in particular public buildings, must give something more to the people who inhabit them than simply meeting functional, technological, and environmental objectives. Of course they must meet the base requirements, whether it's a great place to play badminton, to learn to swim, to dance or to read books, and that they must consume less energy and use fewer resources is a must—but they need to offer *more*. As architects of public buildings we bear a responsibility to create buildings that provide joy, that provide access to all and beyond this encourage anyone and everyone to enter, to feel welcome and equal, to stay longer, to start a conversation…and to reach the top of the pyramid.

There were many questions explored during the course, and discoveries made along the way that have both impacted and validated our approach to architecture. Social sustainability will continue to be an exciting and central part of our practice, along with asking questions and seeking answers.

Student project: Laura Dolson Student project: Raneen Nosh Student project: Shauna Breslawski

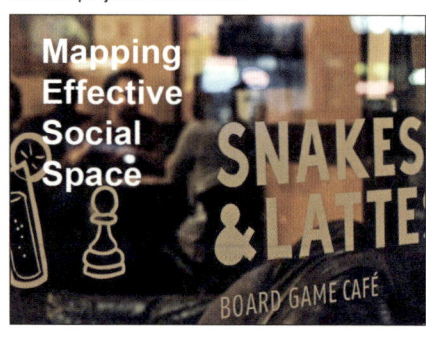  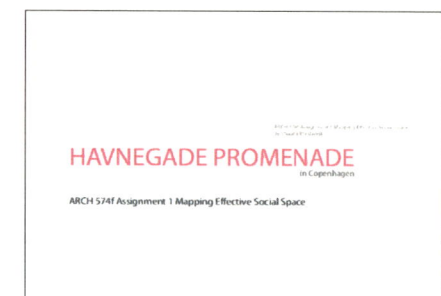

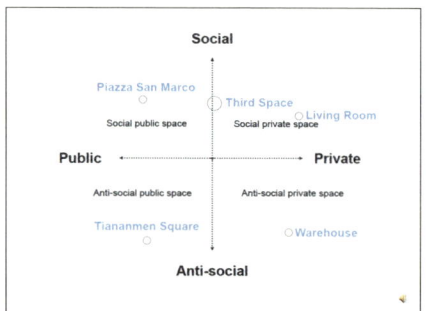  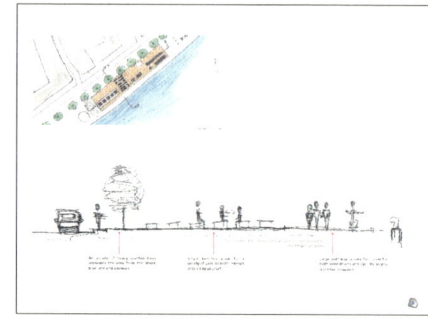

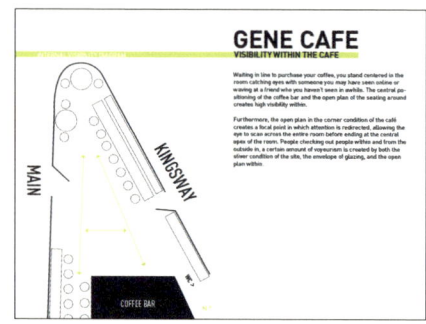 

UniverCity Childcare
Burnaby, BC

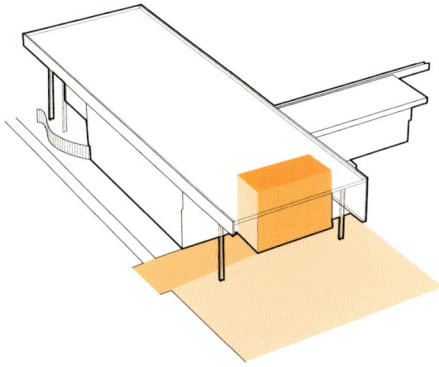

Client
SFU Community Trust

Year
2012

Size
530 m²

Certification
Targeting Living Building Challenge certification

Awards
2013 CaGBC National Leadership Green Building Champion Award
2013 Canadian Society of Landscape Architects Award of Excellence
2012 City of Burnaby Environment Award, Planning and Development
2012 UDI Awards for Excellence, Best Sustainable
2012 Prime Minister's Awards for Excellence in Early Childhood Education

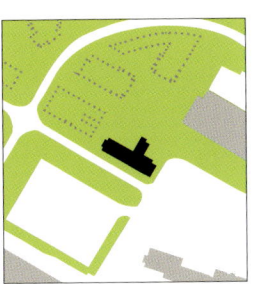

Dating from the creation of the university in the mid-1960s, the client for this project, the SFU Community Trust holds the development rights to 320 hectares of Burnaby Mountain. The Trust uses the profits from its market developments in the surrounding UniverCity sustainable neighbourhood to fund public facilities that will showcase leading edge green design.

On this occasion, the Trust chose to embrace the Living Building Challenge (LBC), which aims to create a symbiotic relationship between the built and natural environments, and overcome the obstacles that currently prevent the realization of these synergies. The childcare centre became only the seventh building in the world to register for the LBC.

The building occupies a sloping site; its L-shaped plan allows for grade access to the main entry on the low side, and from the playground to the upper floor on the high side. To the north and south are separate "learning centres", one double height and oriented to the street and greater community, the other a single storey space that extends into the hillside along one edge of the large outdoor play area. This area includes several unique play structures designed by local artisans.

Internally, the two learning centres meet at a common kitchen and washroom area, and together these spaces constitute the basic minimum program requirement for a Ministry of Education daycare facility. However, through careful design and within the prescribed budget, an additional community space has been created to the west with steps leading to a mezzanine that overlooks the learning centres.

The varied character of the interior spaces, accentuated by the careful use of natural light, encourages a broad range of activities, from individual study to group performances. The program organization also ensures the integration of each classroom with the rest of the school and the school with the surrounding community. These interfaces are carefully articulated at the scale of the child.

With its lightness of touch, the centre successfully captures the spirit of pre-design workshops in which the children expressed their aspirations for the building, including a desire to "climb high" and "play with water." This approach resonates emphatically with the Reggio Emilia philosophy of early childhood education embraced by the daycare staff.

Named for the Italian city in which it was first developed, Reggio Emilia is an educational pedagogy that emphasizes the value of the environment and the community in fostering the physical, social, and emotional development of young children. As a testament to the transformative power of this philosophy, the local elementary school has chosen to adopt the Reggio Emilia method as a result of its experience with the first young graduates from the childcare centre.

BOTTOM Rendered section showing the interconnectedness of spaces, as wel as solar hot water roof s ystem well.
OPPOSITE BOTTOM The design team held a workshop with children to determine "What makes a great play environment?" The results of that workshop influenced the outdoor play spaces which are rich in experiential qualities.

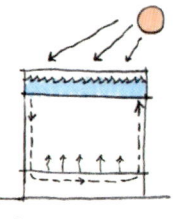
SOLAR HOT WATER

POWER FROM WIND

GEOTHERMAL

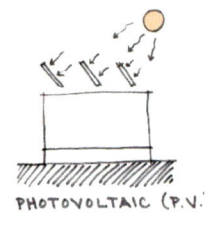
PHOTOVOLTAIC (P.V.)

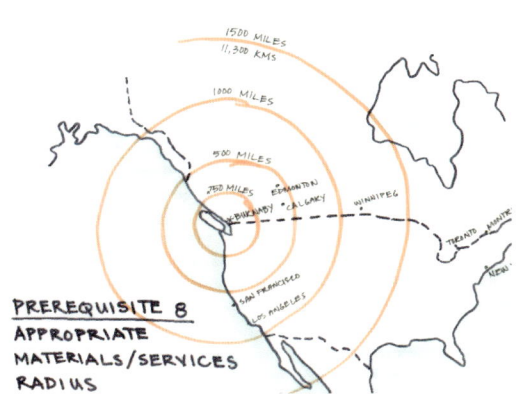
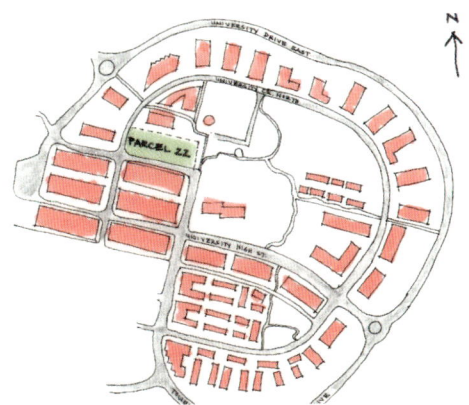
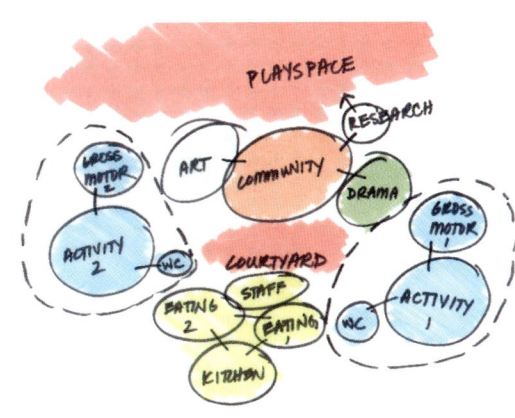

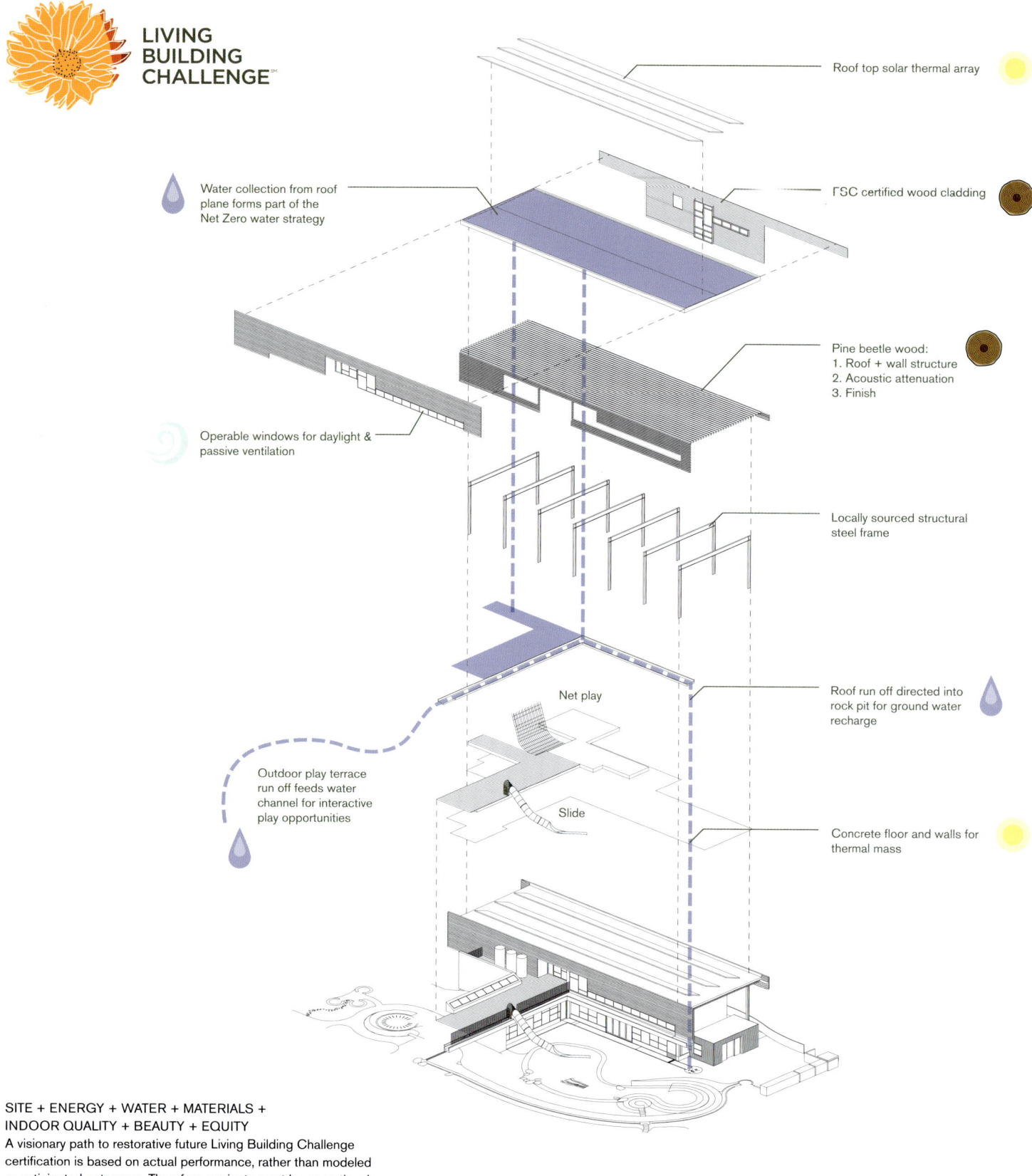

LIVING BUILDING CHALLENGE

- Roof top solar thermal array
- FSC certified wood cladding
- Water collection from roof plane forms part of the Net Zero water strategy
- Pine beetle wood:
  1. Roof + wall structure
  2. Acoustic attenuation
  3. Finish
- Operable windows for daylight & passive ventilation
- Locally sourced structural steel frame
- Roof run off directed into rock pit for ground water recharge
- Outdoor play terrace run off feeds water channel for interactive play opportunities
- Net play
- Slide
- Concrete floor and walls for thermal mass

SITE + ENERGY + WATER + MATERIALS + INDOOR QUALITY + BEAUTY + EQUITY

A visionary path to restorative future Living Building Challenge certification is based on actual performance, rather than modeled or anticipated outcomes. Therefore, projects must be operational for at least twelve consecutive months prior to evaluation.

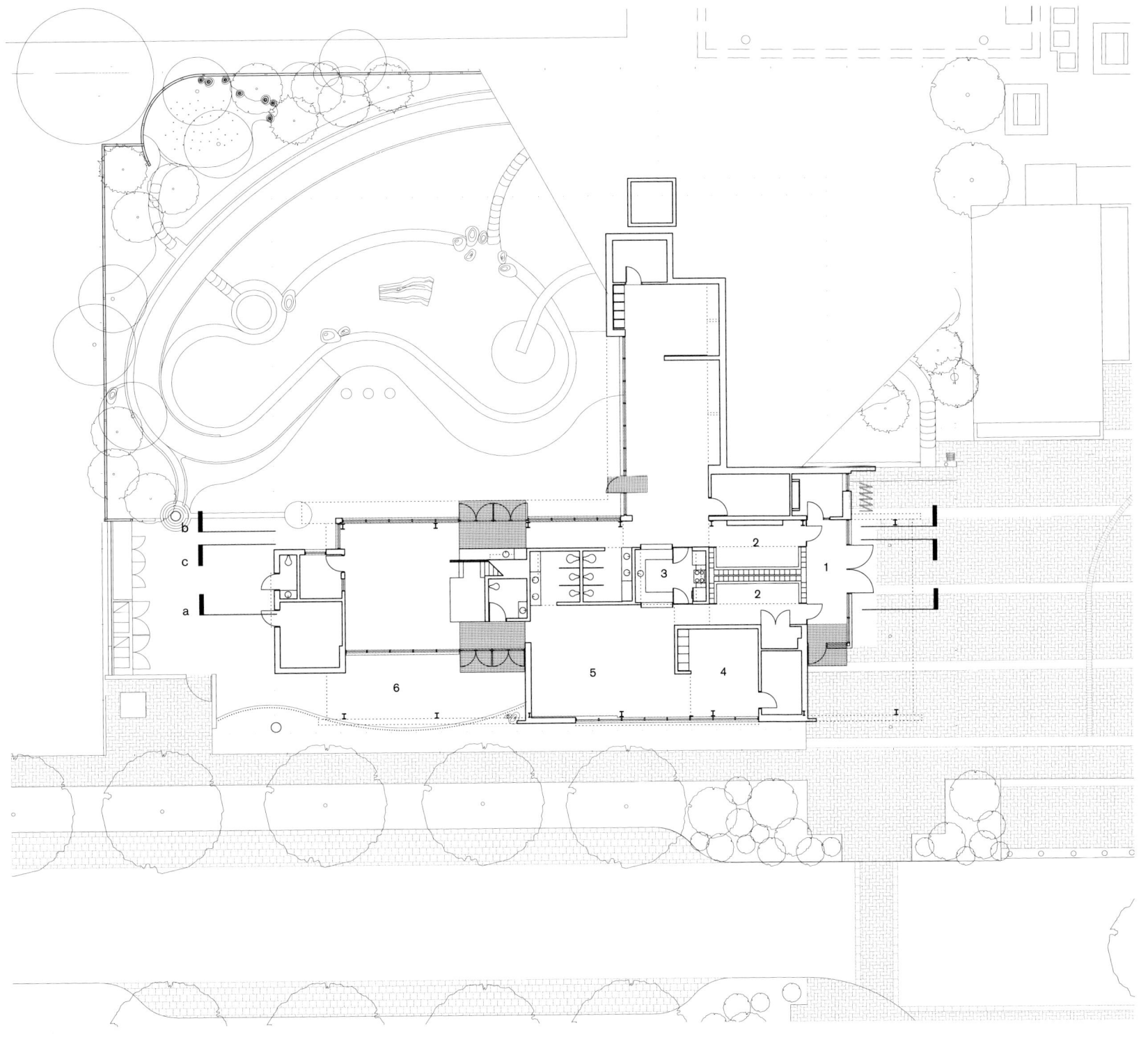

1 Lobby
2 Cubbies
3 Kitchen
4 Gross Motor Nap Room
5 South Activity Room
6 Covered outdoor Play Area

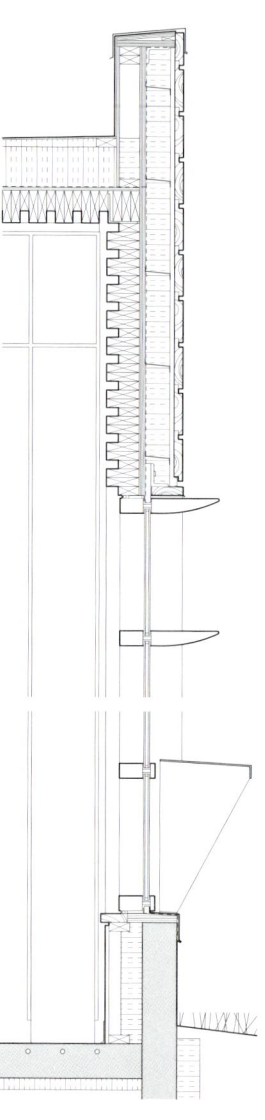

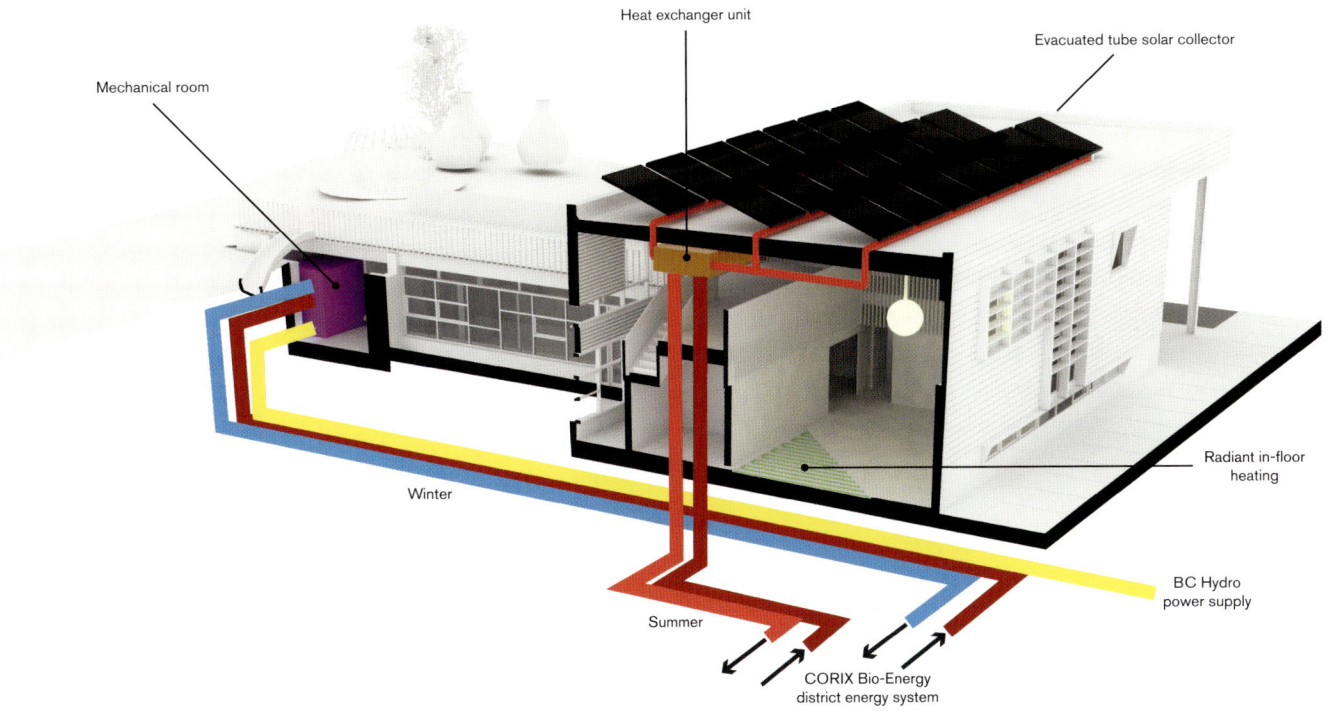

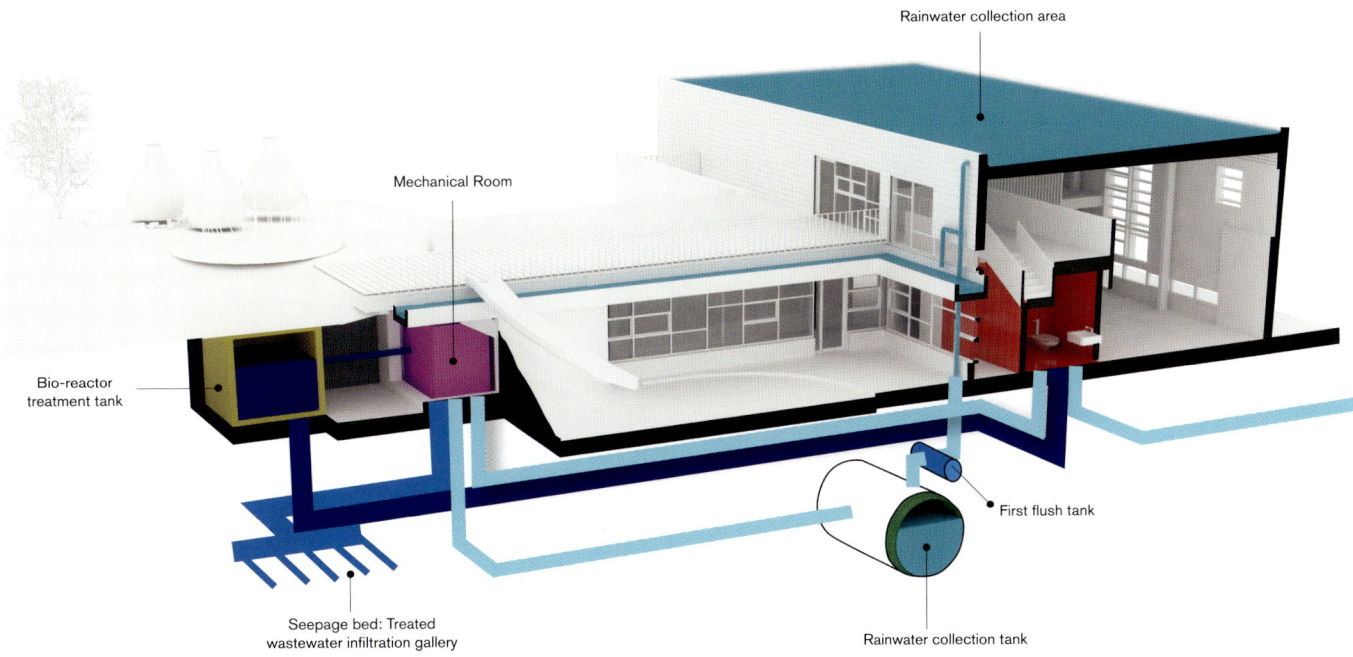

THIS PAGE TOP Net-zero energy system
THIS PAGE BOTTOM Water system

INPUT

- Municipal potable water (required by code)
- Rainwater → Storage Tank

USE

ON-SITE

KITCHEN
- DISHWASHER
- DRINKING FOUNTAIN
- SINK (INCLUDING JANITORIAL)

BATHROOM
- SINK
- TOILET FLUSHING

SUPPORT
- LAUNDRY

LANDSCAPE
- IRRIGATION
- WATER FEATURES

- Water treatment system
- Underground infiltration system
- Underground infiltration galleries

OUTPUT

- City sewer system (required by code, but not used)
- Aquifer / Ground
- UniverCity stormwater system

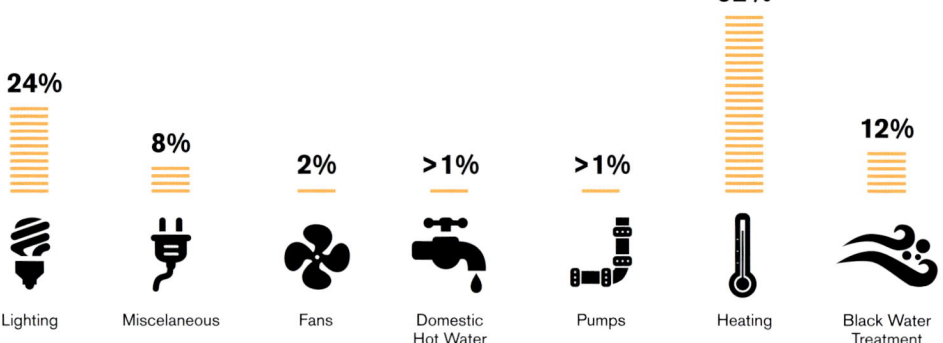

24%	8%	2%	>1%	>1%	52%	12%
Lighting	Miscelaneous	Fans	Domestic Hot Water	Pumps	Heating	Black Water Treatment

OPPOSITE TOP Water management flow diagram showing extensive on-site uses. OPPOSITE BOTTOM Each icon describes the proportion of energy used by each building system required for the facility's operation.

RIGHT Local artist Alastair Heseltine created woven willow play huts as play spaces of different scale in the playground. Collaboration with local artists formed a series of imaginative indoor and outdoor play environments specifically designed for the centre to inspire exploration, imagination, and a sense of wonder.

View from a quiet nap space out to the double-height group play and learning space. The window sills and furnishings are designed for the experience and scale of the child, and are intended to encourage interaction with their environment.

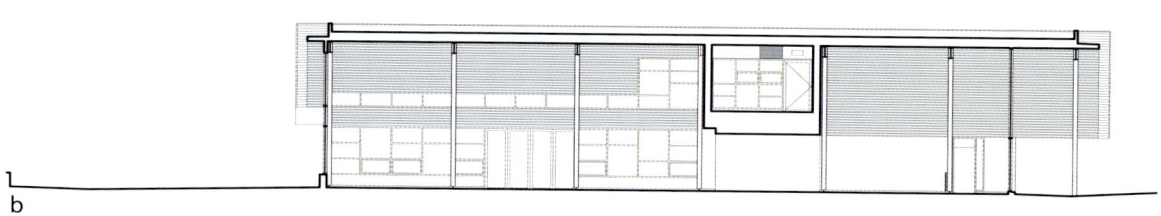

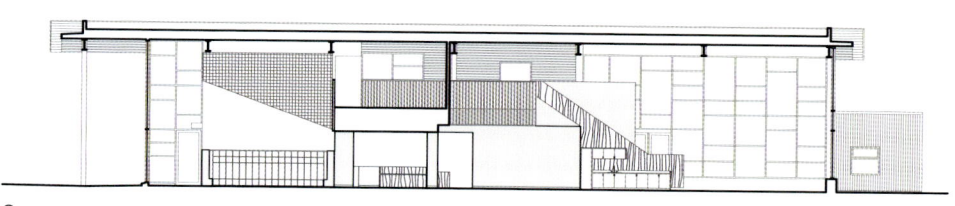

b

c

21 Community Loft Space
22 Staff Lounge
23 Mechanical Room
24 Net Play Space
25 Deck

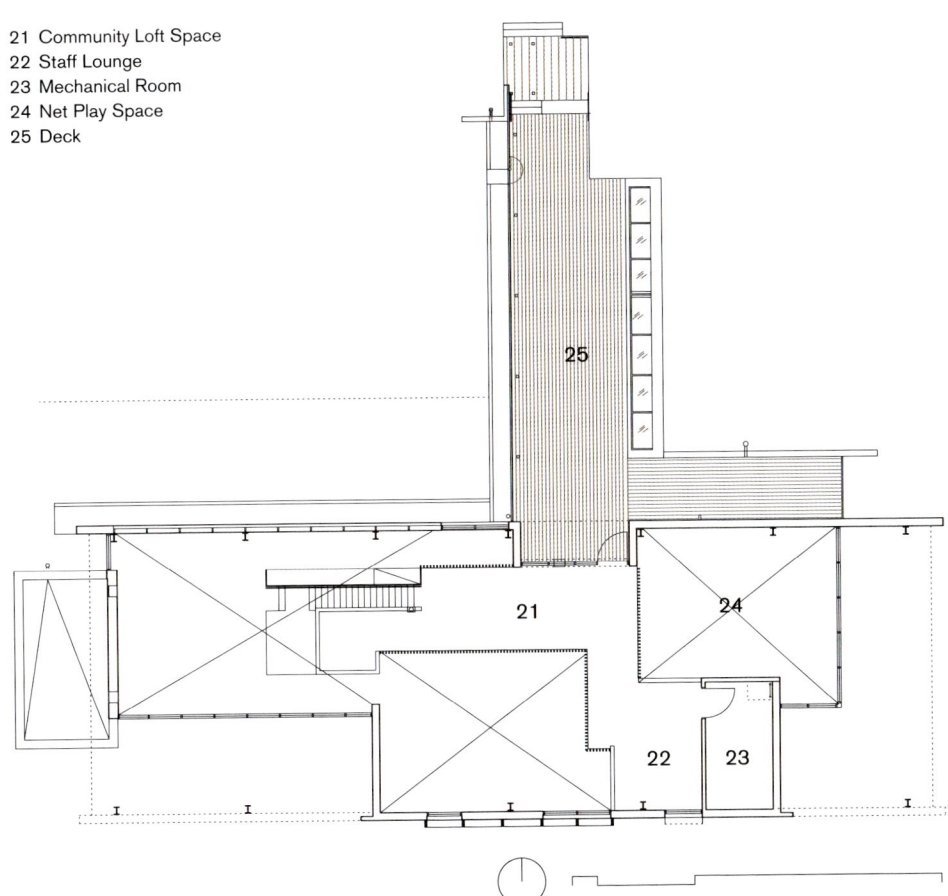

The extensive pinebeetle-damaged wood wall and ceiling finish is a creative space- and cost-saving design solution. It provides acoustic treatment, simultaneously acts as a finish, frame and diaphram, and provides a warm interior finish for the childcare program.

The open, interconnected spaces provide visual access across the extent of the centre, welcoming daylight into the spaces and allowing for passive ventilation.

JASPER PLACE

Jasper Place Library
Edmonton, AB

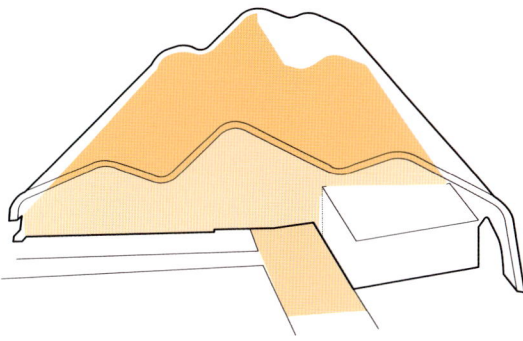

Client
City of Edmonton

Year
2012

Size
1,400 m²

Awards
2014 Prairie Design Awards
2013 Edmonton Urban Design Award of Merit
2013 World Architecture Festival Shortlist - Culture Category
2011 Chicago Athenaeum / European Centre for Architecture - International Award

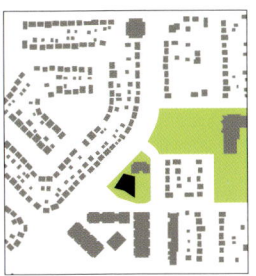

"What is a library that has no books?"

Jasper Place was HCMA's first opportunity to address this most contemporary of questions in physical terms. The project replaces an earlier branch library that was located on the same site. The client's goal was to create a new social heart within an older suburban neighbourhood while providing a flexible building that would be responsive to the rapid changes currently taking place within the delivery of library services.

The building form is defined by a dramatic undulating concrete roof that rises from the ground plane in a gesture of shelter in this harsh northern climate. The roof creates a single large interior space that is the social heart of the building as well as the community. The needs of the social spaces were given priority in the planning with the collections being used to define and enhance the social spaces.

The undulations of the roof, and the careful control and articulation of natural light, create differing characters and spatial conditions that help to define a variety of uses. The main space incorporates a continuous raised floor that provides flexibility for reconfiguration over time and eliminates the need for services at roof level. This ground floor plane of social spaces "folds up" to form a mezzanine, beneath which are tucked the "back of house" functions including the administrative offices and an automated book sorting area. These support spaces are positioned so that the spaces can be converted to public uses as the needs of the collection evolve over time.

Two sets of stairs (one of which also doubles as an informal meeting place and amphitheater) are located at either end of the mezzanine and form a continuous circulation loop. Individual bar style seating offers a place to perch with views to the street, and an outdoor terrace above the main entrance extends the public space at the south side of the building.

While books may not completely disappear from our libraries, it is clear that the size and nature of the collections they house is changing, and that within the life span of this building the needs of the collection will be very different than they are today. Already e-books and the ever expanding amount of information accessible on-line has resulted in a reduction of the size of the physical book collection—even though the area of the new library is twice that of the building it replaced. This technological revolution has transformed libraries from being primary repositories of information and places for private study to conduits for learning in a social environment.

Jasper Place points to a new definition of the public library as a social focus for the community it serves. The overall result is an open, inviting, memorable, and much-needed public space that provides a strong civic presence in a neighbourhood that has lacked one for too long.

This project was completed in joint venture with Edmonton-based Dub Architects.

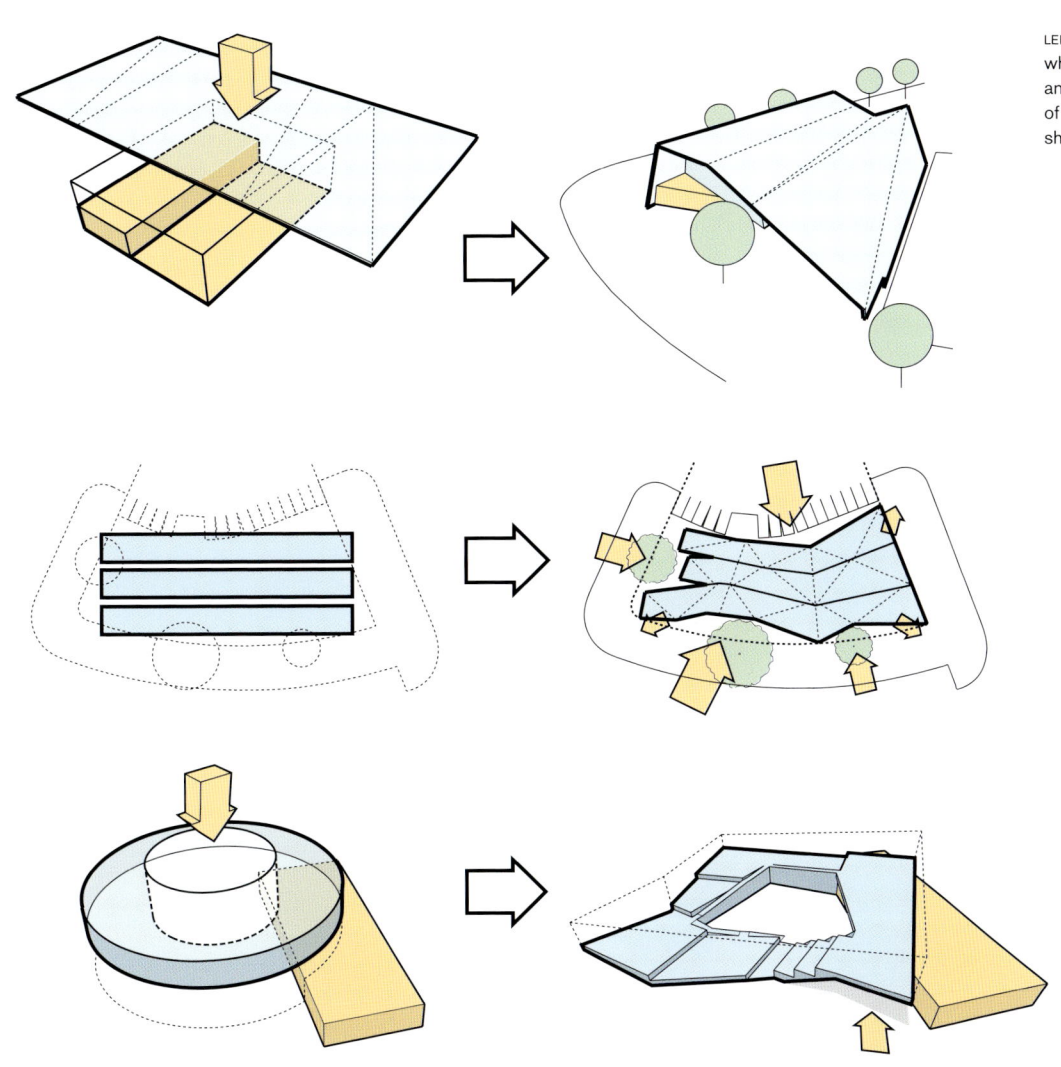

LEFT Early design exploration produced three strong contenders which were called, for case of discussion, the flag, the donut, and the shell. After reviewing the strengths and weaknesses of each strategy with the client it was determined that the shell showed the most promise.

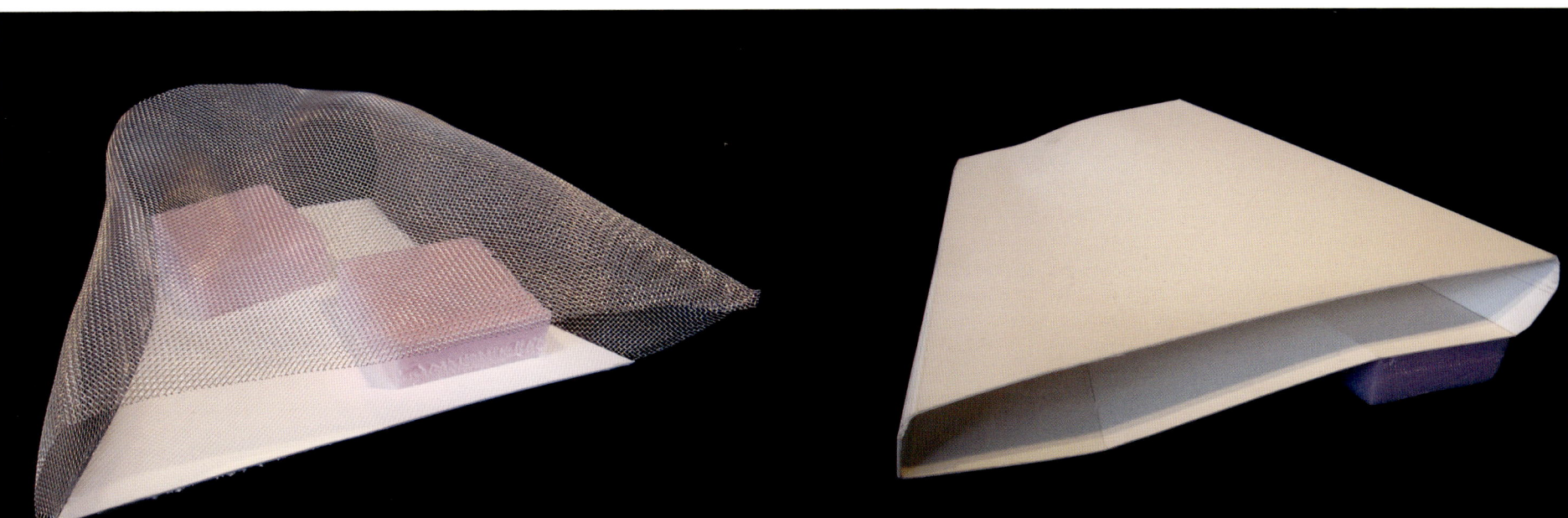

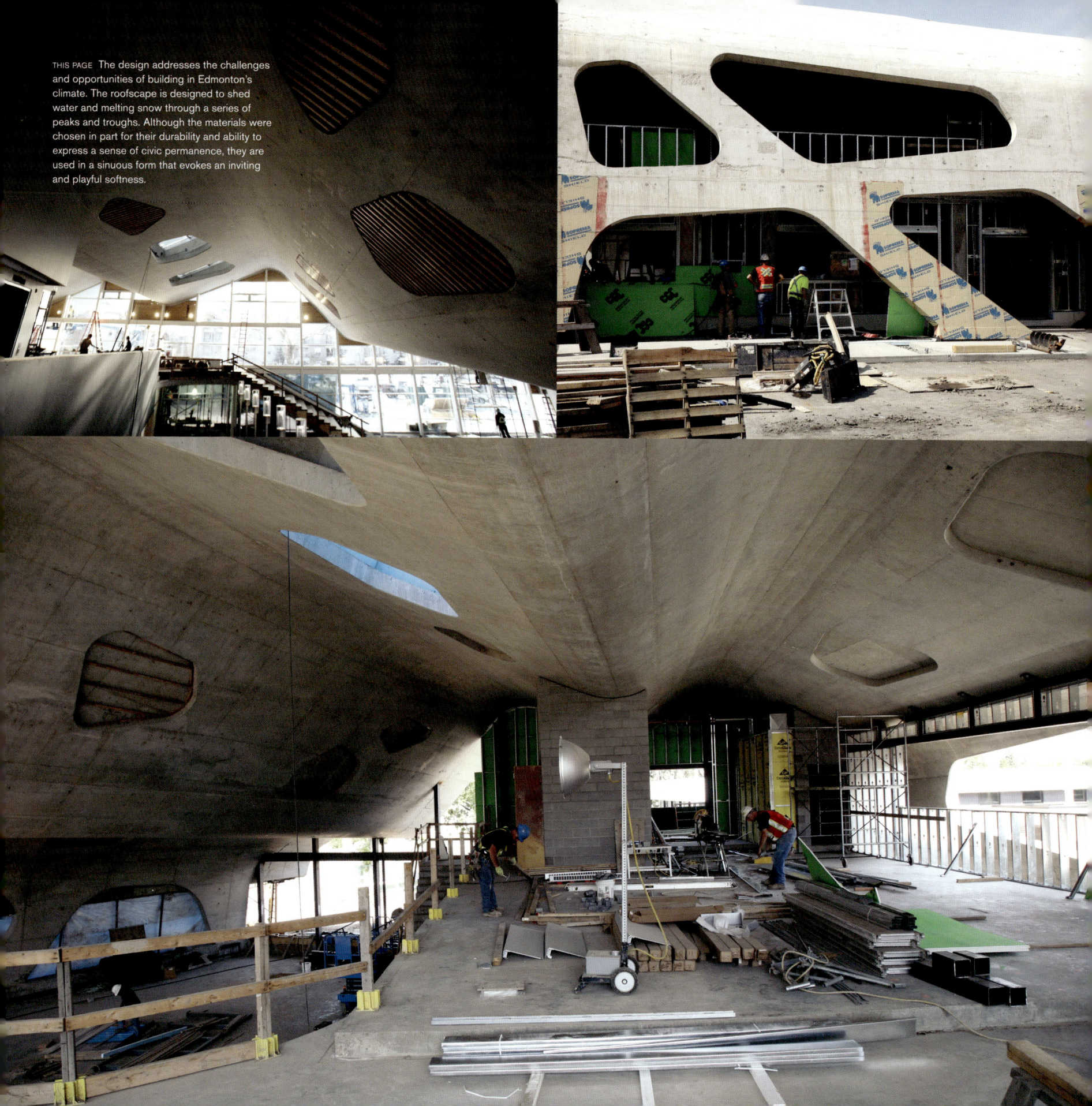

THIS PAGE The design addresses the challenges and opportunities of building in Edmonton's climate. The roofscape is designed to shed water and melting snow through a series of peaks and troughs. Although the materials were chosen in part for their durability and ability to express a sense of civic permanence, they are used in a sinuous form that evokes an inviting and playful softness.

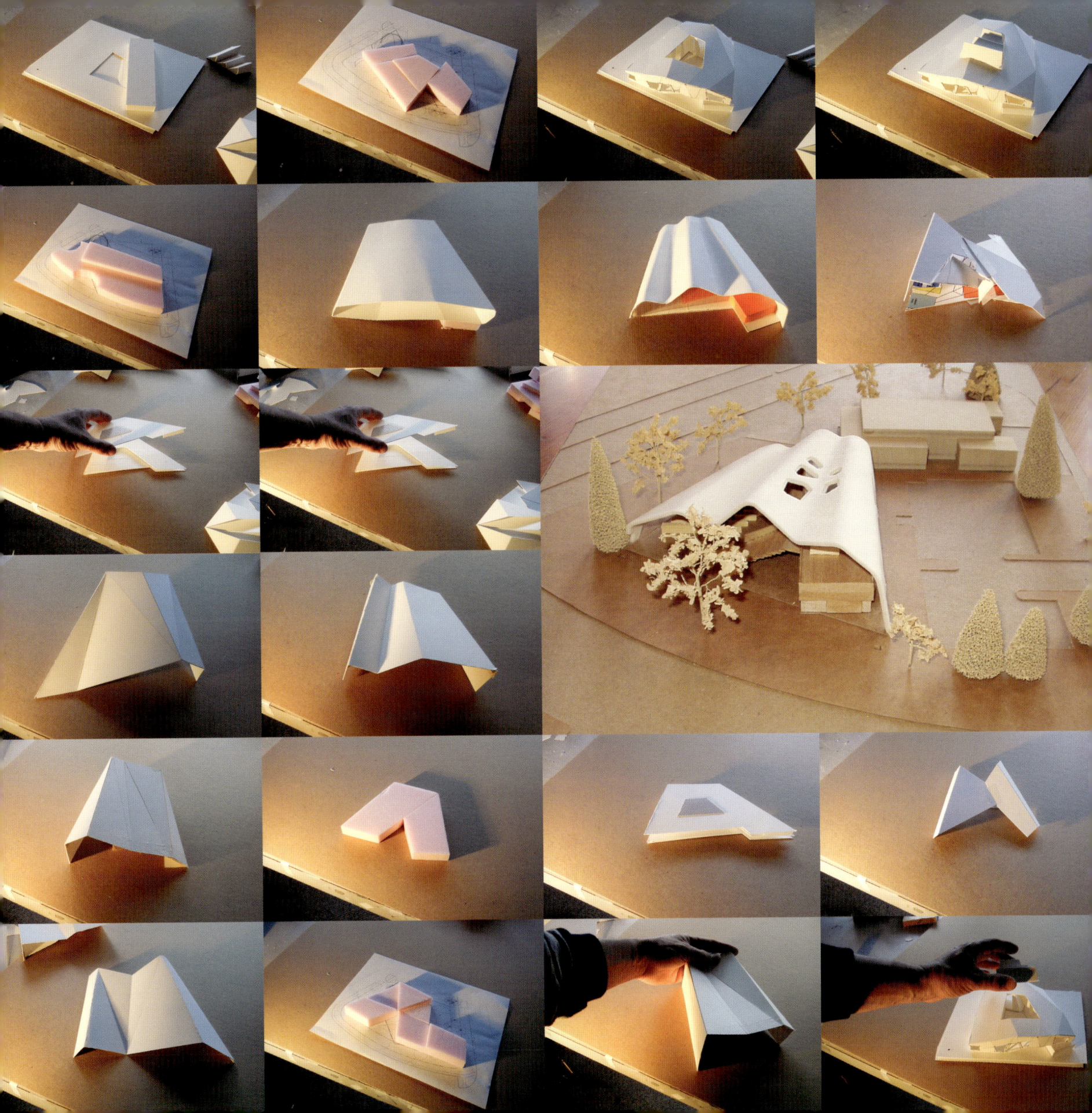

@AdvInFashion
Amazing architecture & furnishings at our new neighbourhood library... #JasperPlace #yeg instagr.am/p/WLB9KwpVw3/
03:28 PM - 25 Feb 13

@shafraaz242
Nice! Striking roof adds grace to new Jasper Place library: How do you make a heavy concrete slab stand without column: bit.ly/112SOWc
05:55 AM - 28 Jan 13

@MirandaDJimmy
Had a chance to visit @EPLdotCA's new #JasperPlace branch on the weekend. Beautiful building inside & out! #YEG pic.twitter.com/Y7aqb2nSDE
07:43 AM - 04 Mar 13

@debhammacher
Visited our FABULOUS new Jasper Place library this week. Love it! Thank you @EPLdotCA and fellow taxpayers.
12:40 PM - 09 Mar 13

@doniveson
Popped by the new Jasper Place @EPLdotCA branch. See - we can have nice things, #yeg. (Soft opened Monday.) #yegcc pic.twitter.com/6T5ei2JaKZ
02:02 PM - 27 Feb 13

@elena_mch
Awesome photo! "@katebusby_: Interior of Edmonton's new #JasperPlace library by @hcma / Dub Architects: 360.io/zJHLgJ"
05:19 PM - 11 Mar 13

@amandaeileenc
the new jasper place library is GORGEOUS. i want to move in asap. #yeg #reno
11:05 AM - 10 Mar 13

@Katanbaf
Jasper Place Branch Library a spaces of social interaction & learning / HCMA/Dub Architects http://bit.ly/15ygMaj pic.twitter.com/YWY8J7MX3m
11:02 AM - 15 Jul 2013

@robinbrittain
Branch Library, Edmonton, AB, Canada. Distinctive undulating roof, flexible open floor plan & predominant glazing: bit.ly/1bgWk41
15 Jul 13

@vatjaiswal
Crazy library in Canada. Archdaily.com/398988/jasper...
12:04 AM - 14 Jul 2013

@SpaceList
What's the coolest library you've ever seen? We think this one in #Edmonton is pretty amazing #CRE – bit.ly/14NwQGs
12 July 13

@cgmonts
Wow they mentioned an Edmonton building "@ArchDaily: Jasper Place Branch Library / HCMA/Dub Architects archdai.ly/1dqP56q #architecture
7:56 AM - 12 Jul 2013

@LuziaAntunes
"In part inspired by the original 1961 Modernist design of the Jasper Place Library, the new 1,400m2 library... fb.me/11ys96oNr
12 July 13

@elena_mch
@hcma & DUB's Jasper Place Library just opened Already up for World Building of the Year 2013 http://goo.gl/08IV3 http://goo.gl/vgqs8
1:14 PM - 3 Jul 2013

@GreatStuffLindy
@IDigYourGF well, if you ever pop into the gorgeous Jasper Place library, be sure to say hello to me!
5:55 PM - 3 Feb 2014

@CaryWilliams
Down the street from us and it is amazing! RT @ETownMickey: Striking roof adds grace to new Jasper Place library http://bit.ly/112SOWc
7:35 PM - 27 Jan 2013

@mpivon
Will this building become a landmark for Jasper Place? - Have you driven past the new Jasper Place library branch an... http://ow.ly/2uu674
4:36 PM - 25 Jan 2013

@RouxBeee
I would go just to see this. Striking roof adds grace to new Jasper Place library http://www.edmontonjournal.com/news/edmonton/
6:21 PM - 27 Jan 2013

@shafraaz242
Love the roof design! New Jasper Place library designed to meet possibly book-free future http://www.edmontonjournal.com/news/Jasper+Place+library+designed+meet+possibly+book+free+future/3510186/story.html?cid=megadrop_story ...
11:33 AM - 11 Sep 2010

THIS PAGE The design was in part inspired by the original 1961 modernist design of the Jasper Place Library and that period when the community was growing. The flexible space will be able to accommodate future reorganizations of the collection and reading areas.

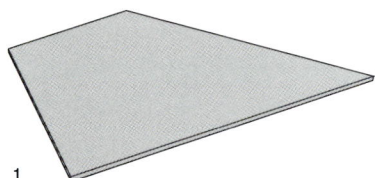
1

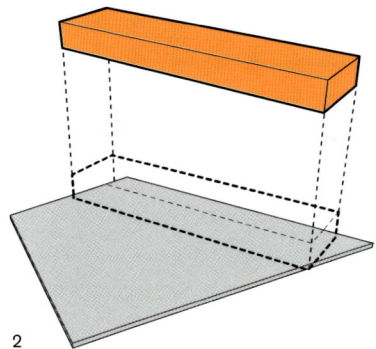
2

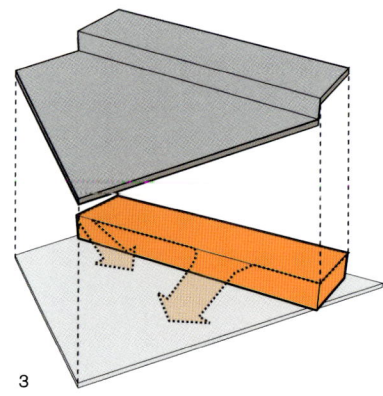
3

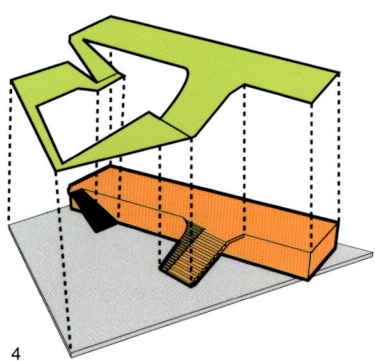
4

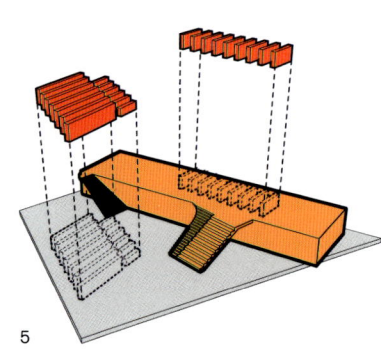
5

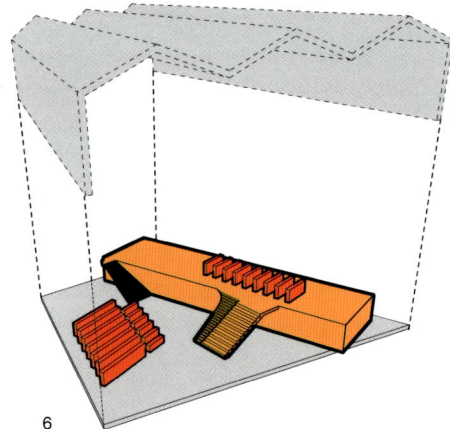
6

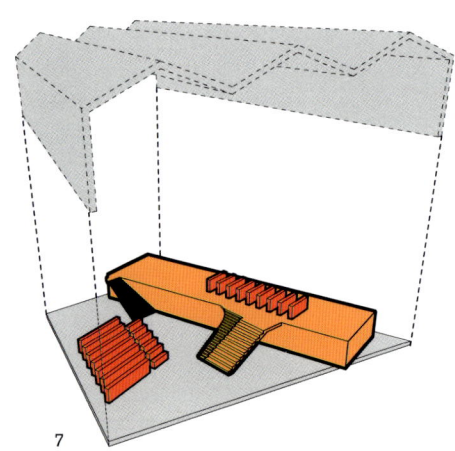
7

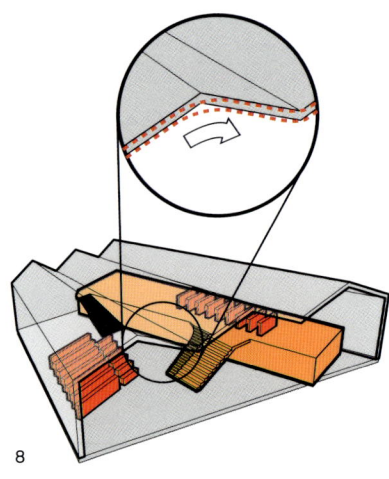
8

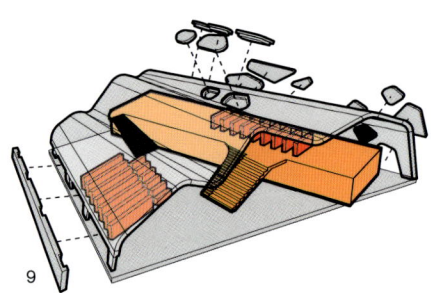
9

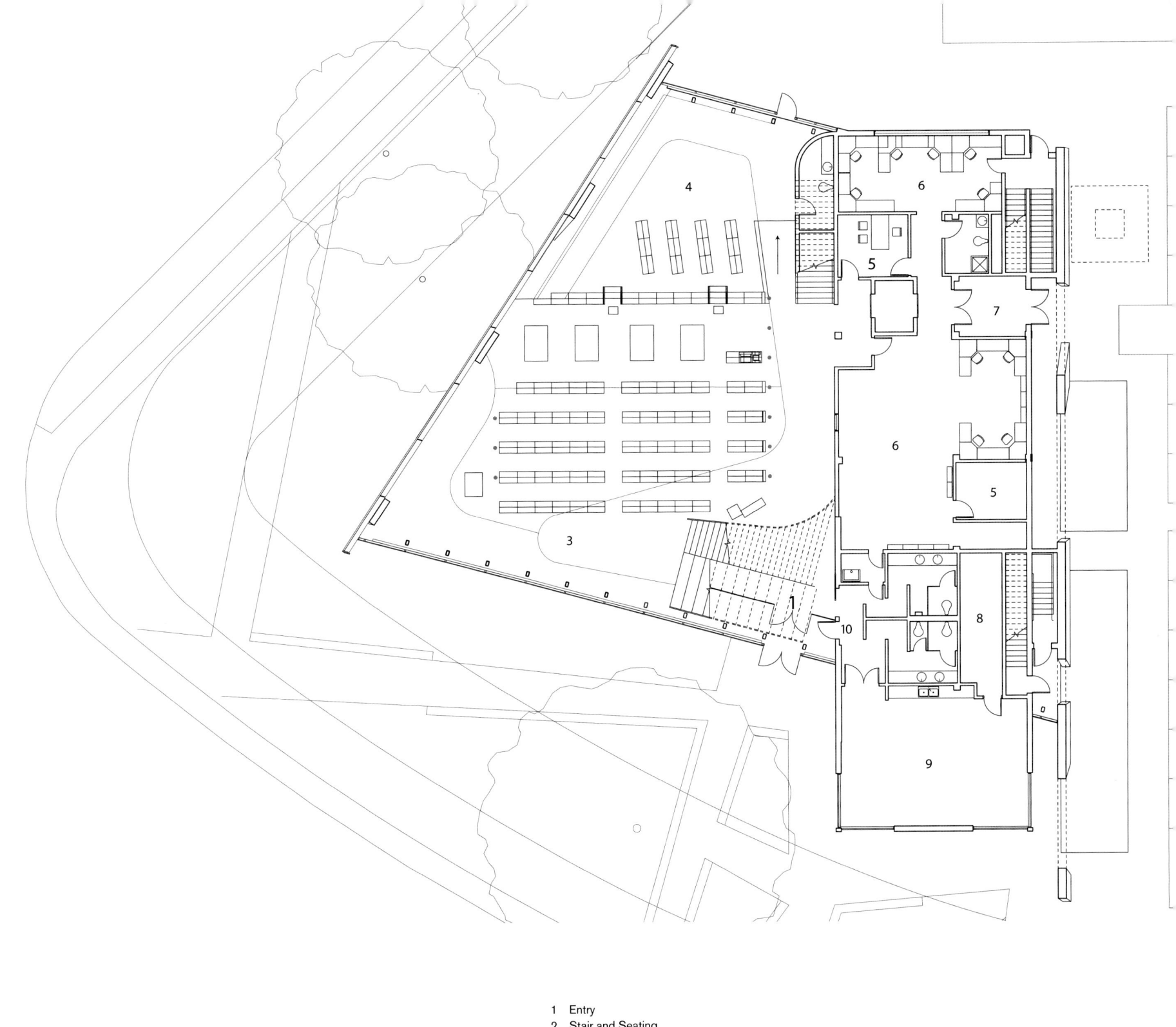

1. Entry
2. Stair and Seating
3. Reading
4. Childrens' Area
5. Office
6. Work Room
7. Loading & Delivery
8. Storage
9. Community Room
10. Washroom

BOTTOM Jasper Place Library expresses civic pride and celebrates structural honesty with a distinctive roofscape and strong profile set against the prairie sky and surrounding trees. OPPOSITE PAGE The Community Room is located adjacent to the entrance so it may be used independently after library hours by the community at large.

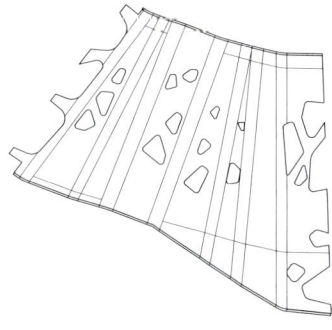
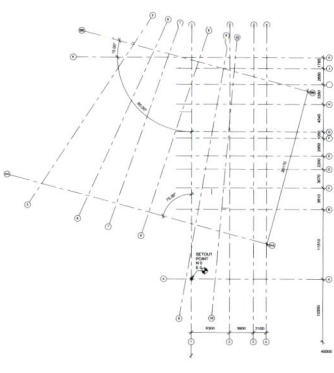
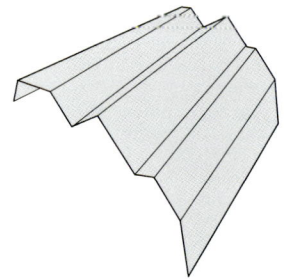
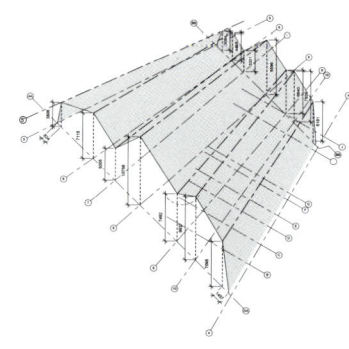

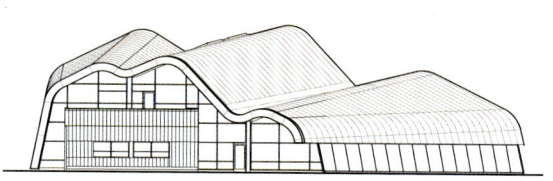

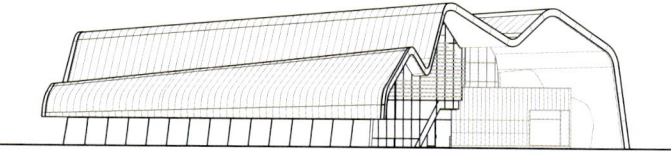
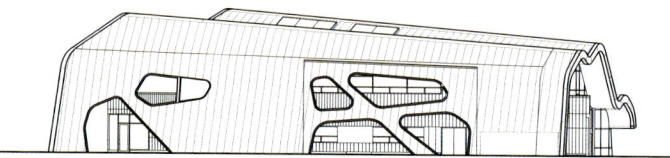

RIGHT The space welcomes all demographics of the community in a distinctive building that announces its unique role in the neighborhood as a place for public use.

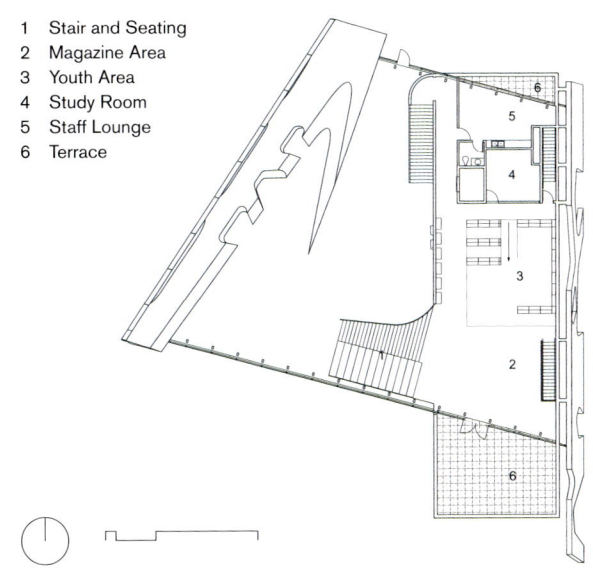

1. Stair and Seating
2. Magazine Area
3. Youth Area
4. Study Room
5. Staff Lounge
6. Terrace

LEFT Stairs (one of which is designed to double as a reading space or an amphitheater) are located at the ends of the mezzanine to form a continuous loop for patrons to circulate.

MILL WOODS

Mill Woods Branch Library, Seniors Centre, and Multicultural Facility
Edmonton, AB

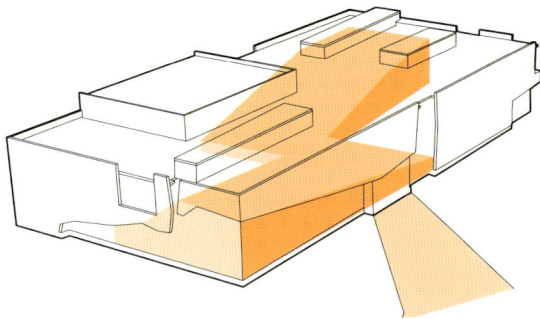

Client
City of Edmonton

Year
2013

Size
4,700 m²

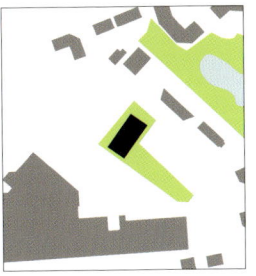

Set within a context of suburban malls and big box retail stores, the challenge was to create a meaningful sense of public space within an ill-defined, utilitarian, and "placeless" environment. HCMA's response to this challenge was to create its own relationships and generate its own context, rather than to respond, or defer, directly to the suburban void space that surrounds the site.

Designed in joint venture with Edmonton based Dub Architects, this project combines a new Public Library together with an integrated Seniors and Multicultural facility.

After a design process that involved a series of both digital and physical models, a formal concept was adopted that juxtaposed solid and void elements combined in a singular form. This creates a play of transparency and opacity that privileges the social spaces of the building. The site design includes a grassy field and a tightly spaced grove of trees, both referencing the local prairie context. This constructed yet highly naturalized setting contrasts with the surrounding generic suburban context.

The primary public spaces of the library area are located within the conceptual void space, making the social functions visible from the exterior. In contrast, the senior/multicultural centre and other semi-private and private spaces are located within the solid volumes. Throughout, social space is prioritized and made deliberately amorphous, as if these spaces were a fluid that flows around the solidly arranged ancillary spaces.

The project provides a critique of the ubiquitous and placeless "big box" stores that have multiplied across North America. Visually, the design employs a material palette similar to its neighbours, yet it refines and recalibrates those materials with a critical approach to detailing. Fundamentally, the project highlights the realities of a lack of true public spaces within many of our communities and its replacement with quasi-public space in shopping centres. Truly democratic spaces that are available to all segments of our society are increasingly rare, and this project seeks for provide a positive alternative.

Within the library, the carefully scaled social spaces are designed to encourage a variety of activities and interactions. Here the typical readings room space is divided into distinct yet linked spaces that expand to the corners of the building visually connecting to the exterior beyond. The dual reading rooms have complementary characters, one responding to the more traditional quiet study, while the other providing a dynamic information commons with a predominance of social space.

The Seniors and Multicultural facility contains smaller scaled and more intimate spaces which respond to the confined nature of these activities and the users need for a more controlled environment. Combined with the library, the entire complex provides a strong cohesive formal concept that asserts itself as an important public building within a context where there are few. In doing so, the project provides a strong social hub in the community.

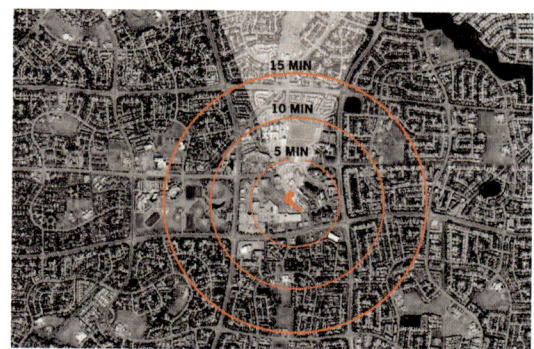

THIS PAGE Site analysis images show the context for which Mill Woods Branch Library, Seniors Centre and Multicultural Facility was developed.

THIS PAGE The diagrams above represent a series of potential options for the footprint of the building which were explored as part of the design process. RIGHT The footprint of Jasper Place Branch Library is placed on the Mill Woods site for comparison with the program area requirements in the diagram below. NEXT SPREAD These study models for Mill Woods quickly explore form, massing, and the relationship between various program components.

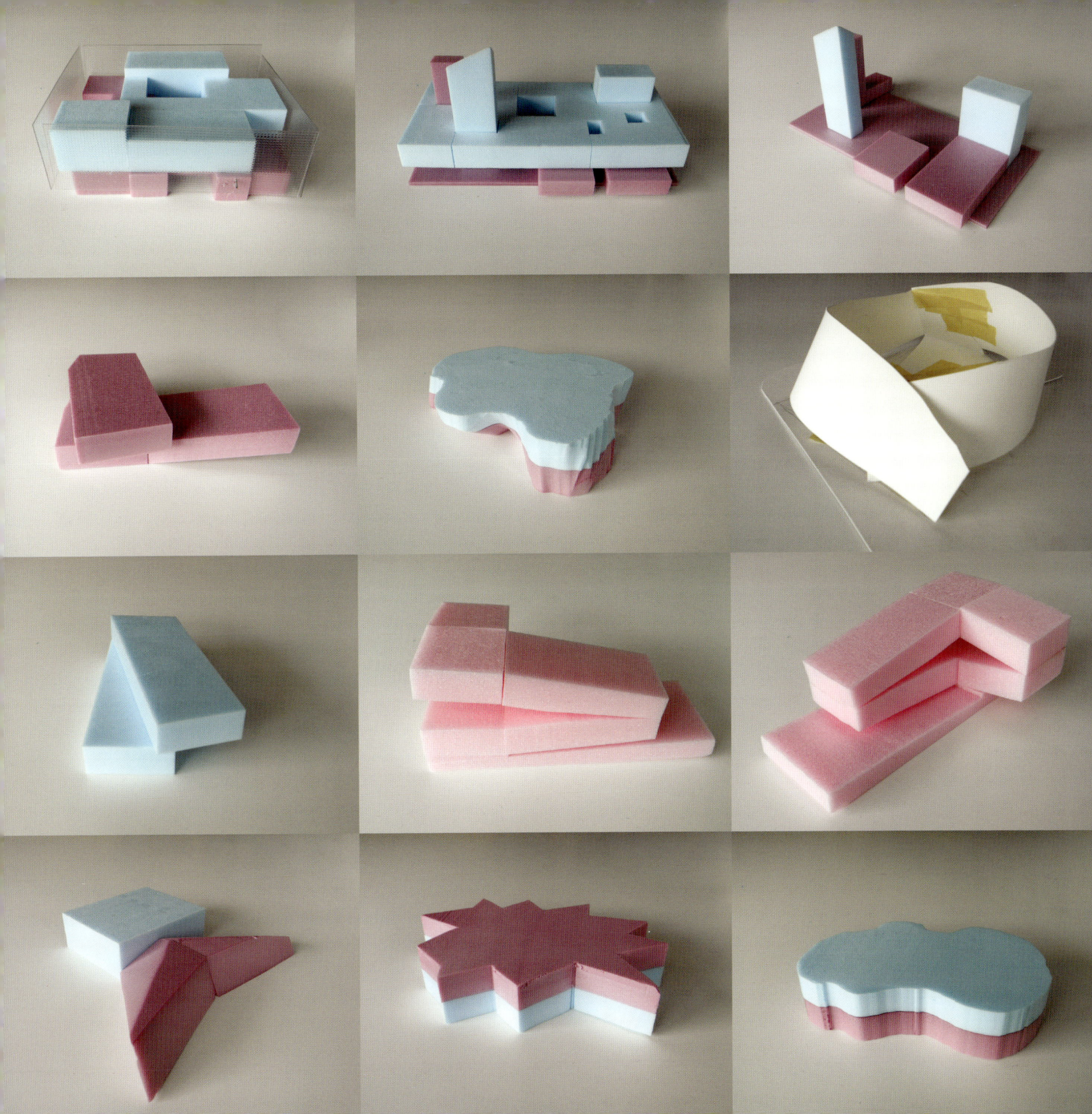

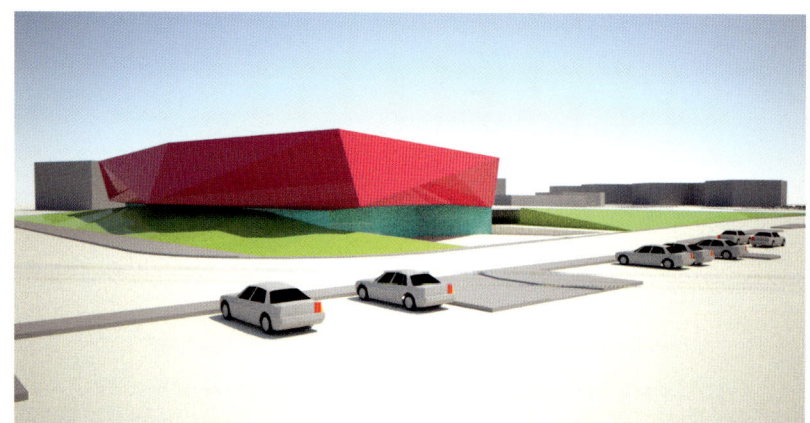
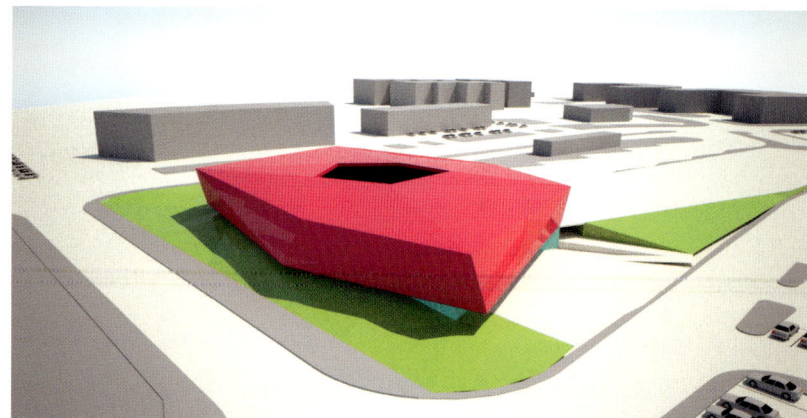
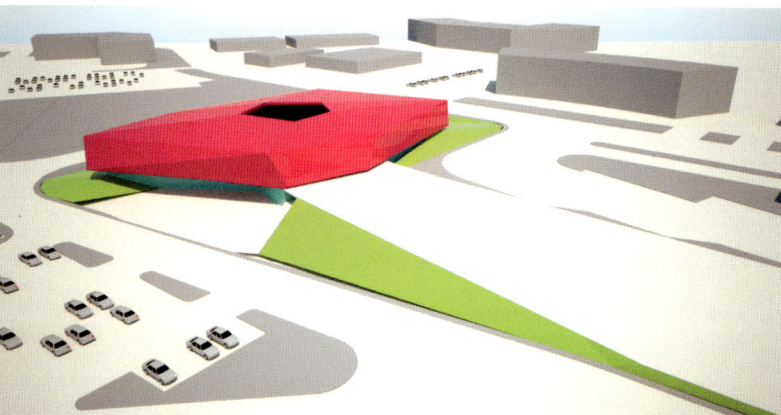

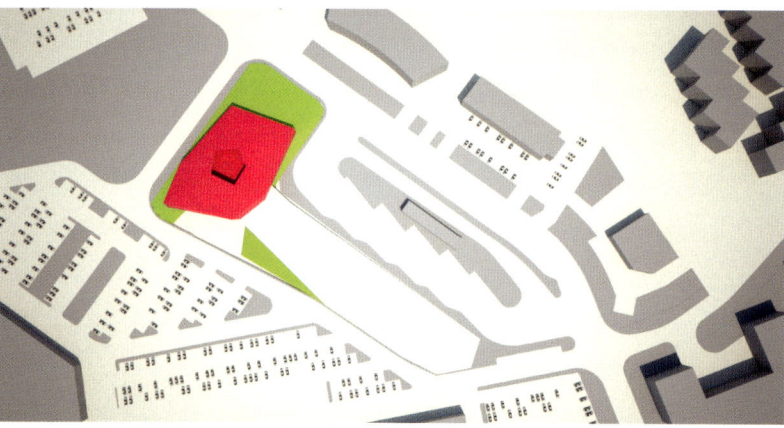

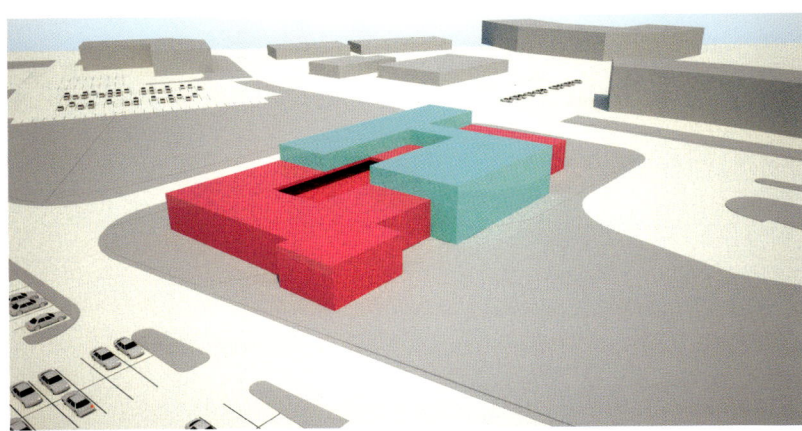
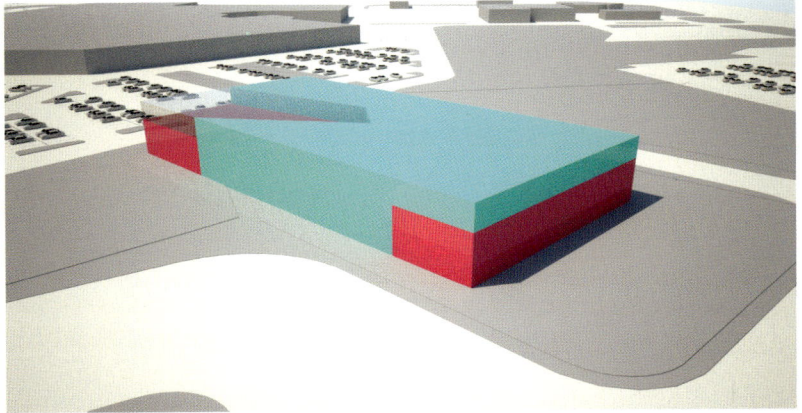
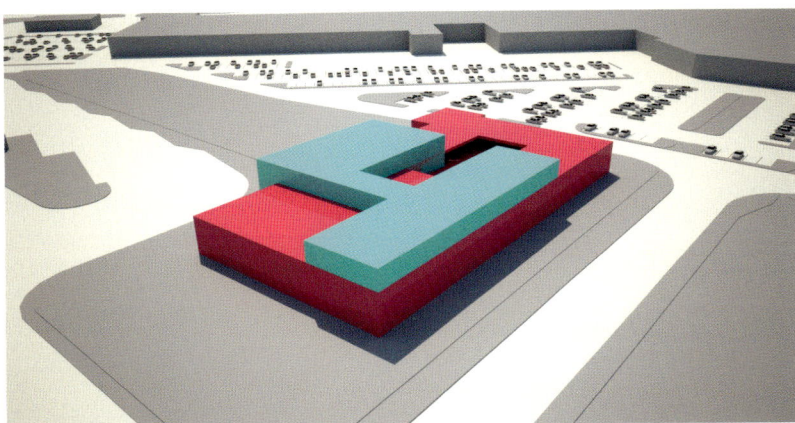
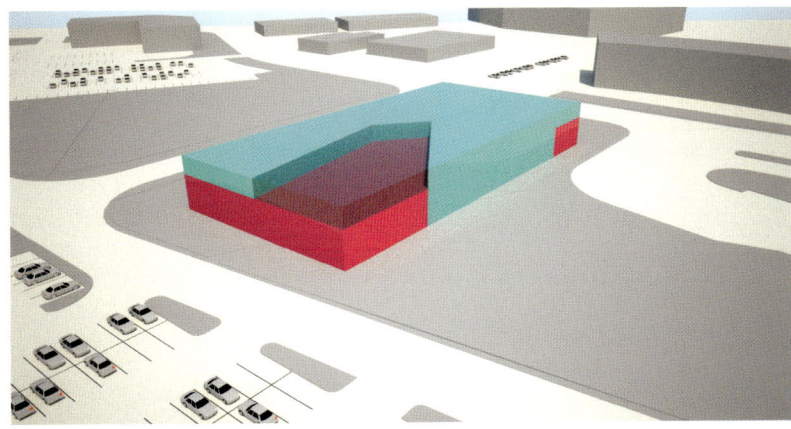
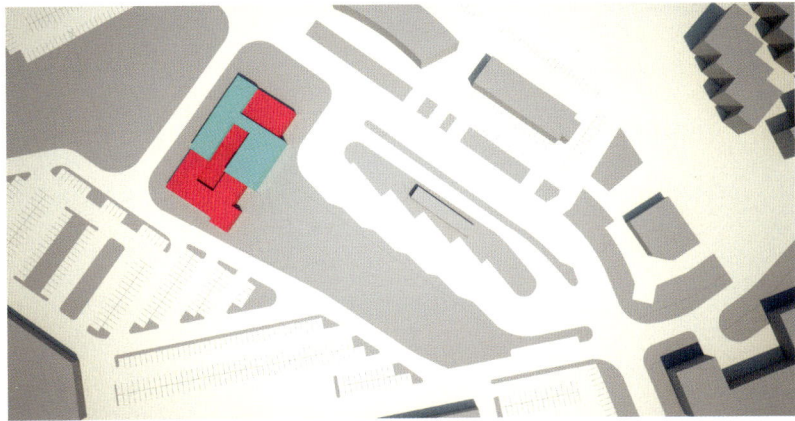

The renders on this spread represent two of the final concepts for the Mill Woods facility. Red and blue colours signify the program designation of the areas within the building.
OPPOSITE PAGE A tessellated jewel form touches down in a carved landscape. ABOVE The volume of a rigorous block is internally carved-out to create an interlocking solid and void space. This concept was selected and developed into the building currently under construction.

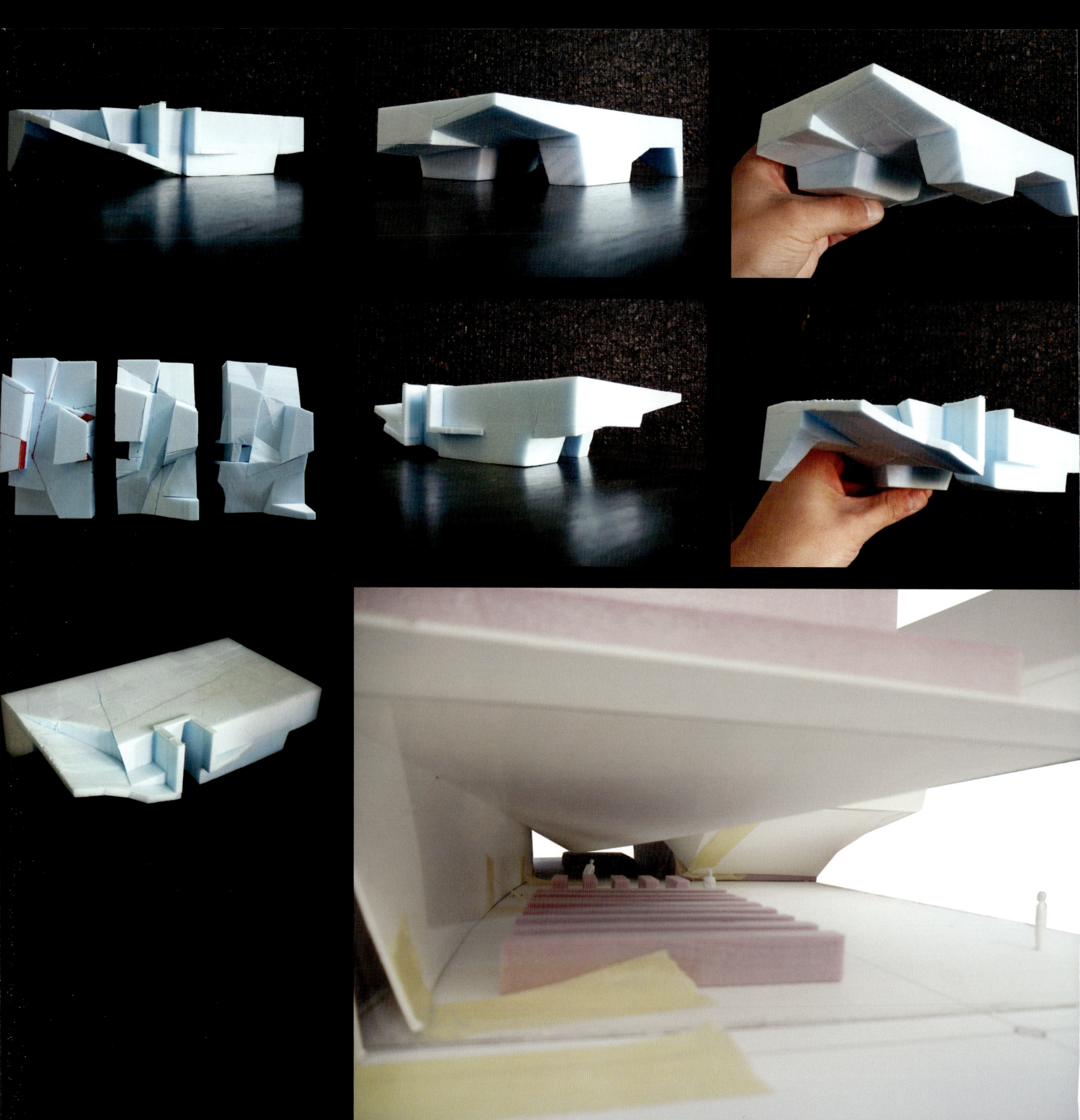

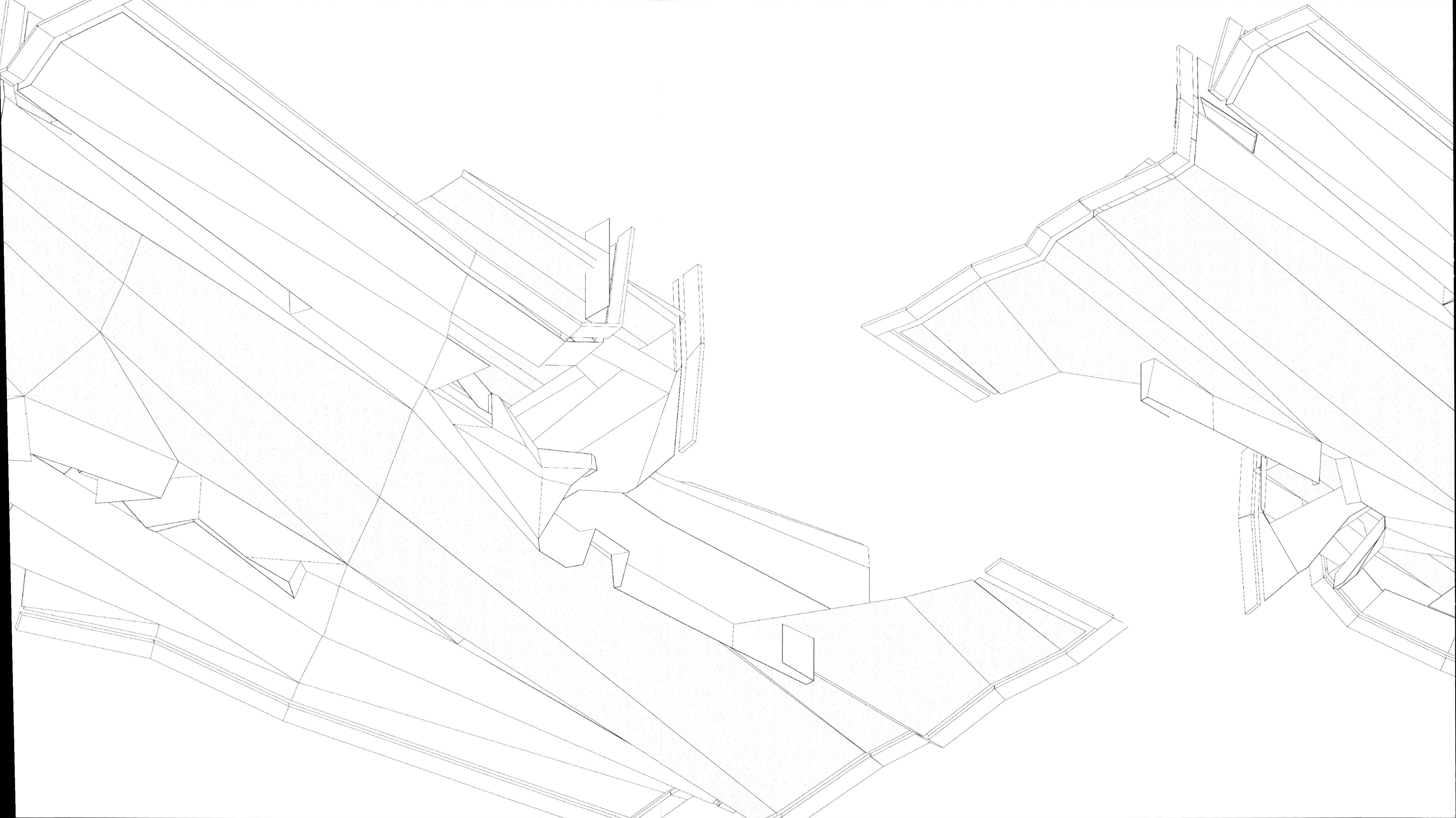

TOP RIGHT The final solid/void concept massing on the Mill Woods site. MIDDLE RIGHT Interlocking solid and void elements. The upper solid blue volume is occupied by the Seniors Centre and Multicultural Facility, while the void white volume contains the branch library.

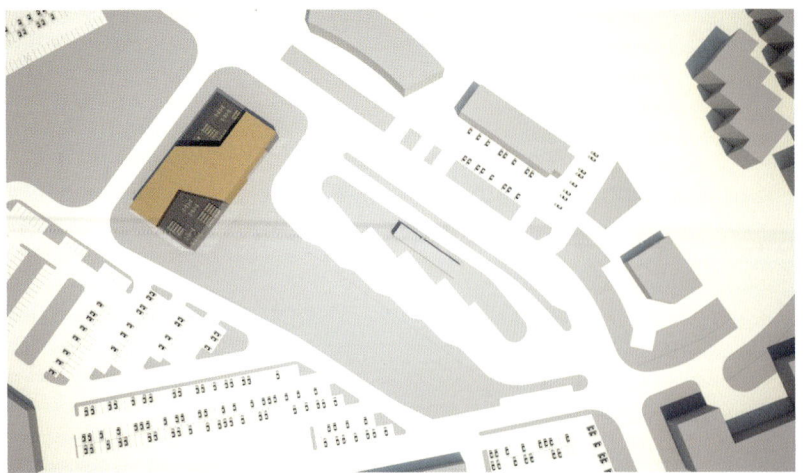

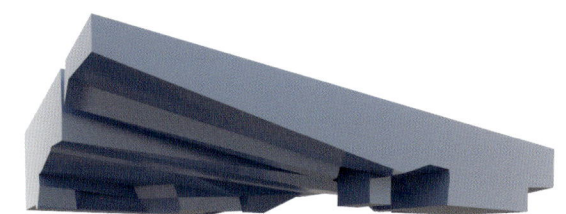

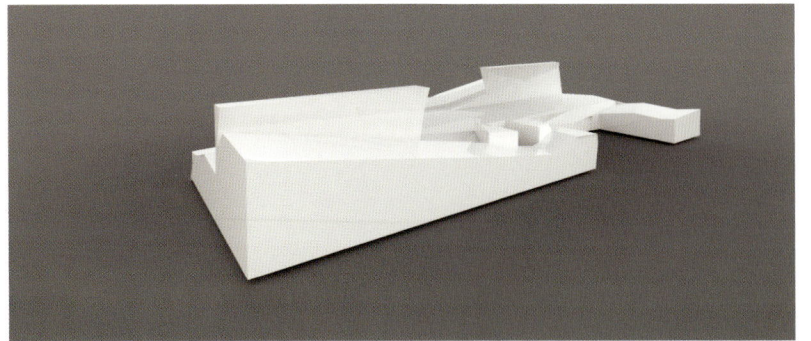

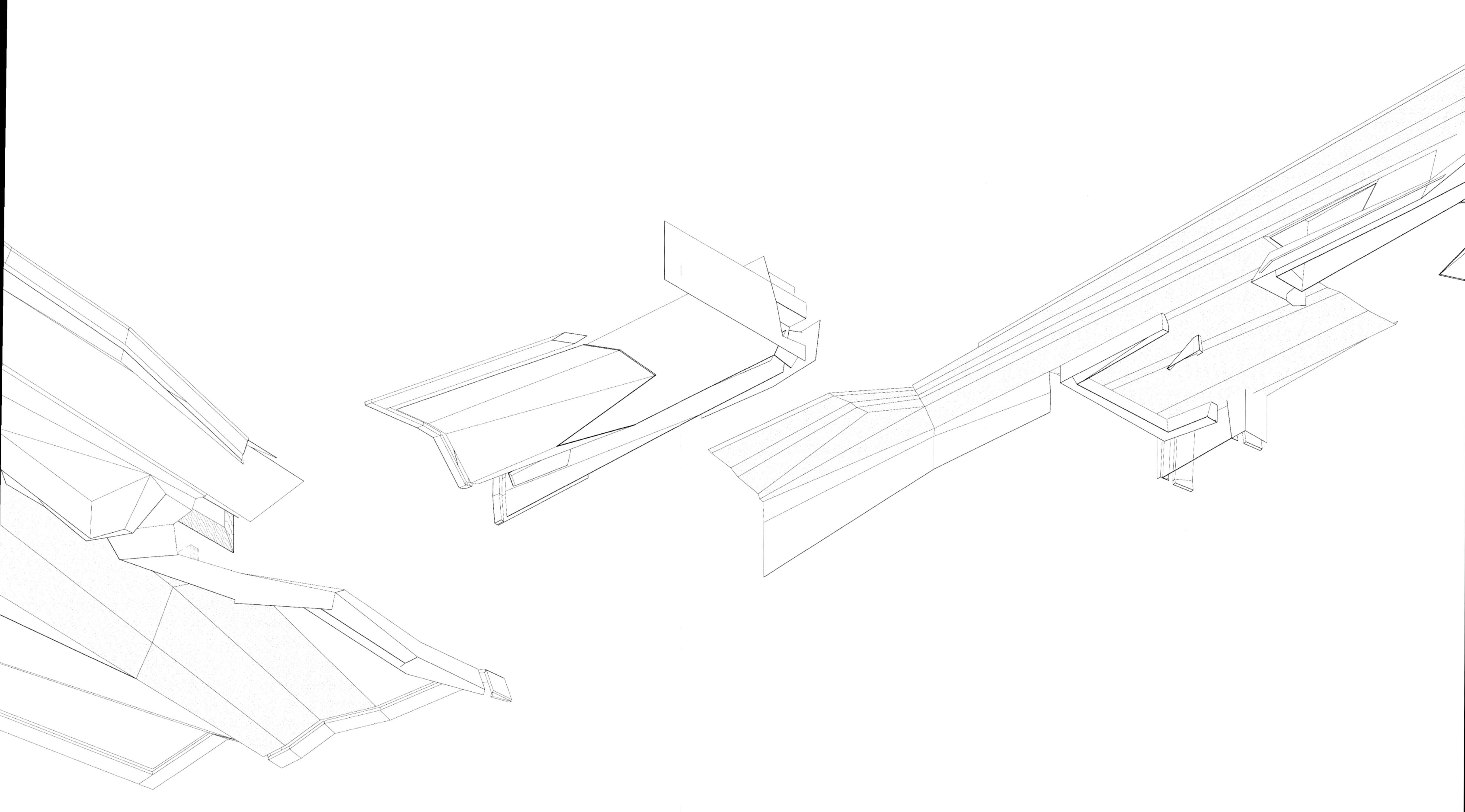

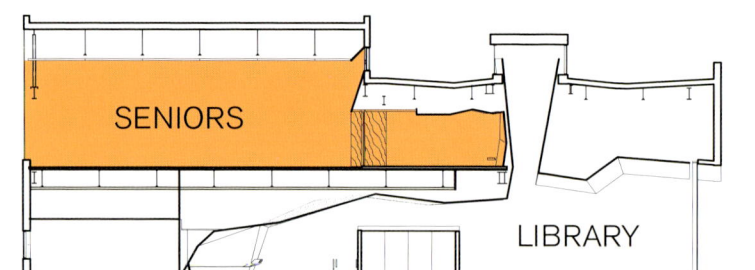
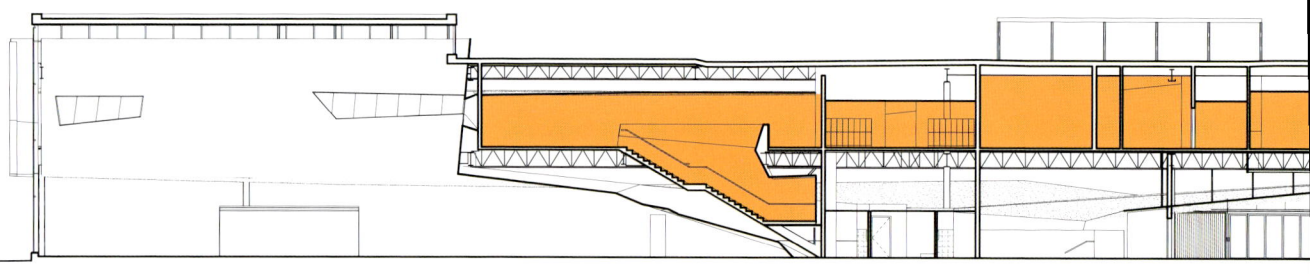
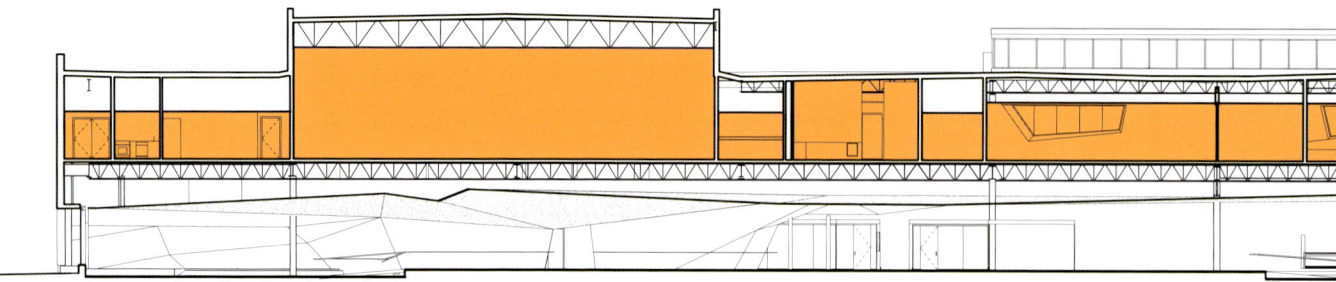

1 Entry
2 West Reading Room
3 Quiet Study
4 West Lower Reading Room
5 Washroom
6 Mechanical/Electrical
7 Community Room
8 East Reading Room
9 East Lower Reading Room
10 Childrens
11 Manager
12 Member Services
13 Work Room
14 Admin Storage
15 Deliveries
16 Library Assistants
17 Staff Lounge

Construction progress photographs show the carved void space (top) and views through sliced openings on the second floor of the solid volume (bottom left and right).

APPENDIX

 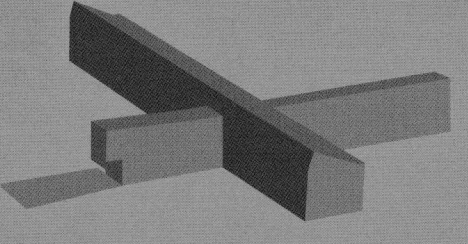 

Whistler Library   **Duchess Park**   **Steveston Firehall**   **UniverCity Childcare**   **Jasper Place**   **Mill Woods**

Project Credits

Whistler Public Library

Client Resort Municipality of Whistler / **Architect of Record** Hughes Condon Marler Architects / **Partner in Charge** Darryl Condon / **Other design team members** Jay Lin, Kurt McLaren, Kayna Merchant, Bill Uhrich / **Structural Engineer** Fast + Epp Structural Engineers / **Mechanical Engineer** Stantec / **Electrical Engineer** Acumen Engineering / **Landscape Architect** Phillips Farevaag Smallenberg / **Contractor** Whistler Construction Company

UniverCity Childcare

Client SFU Community Trust / **Architect of Record** Hughes Condon Marler Architects / **Partner in Charge** Karen Marler / **Other design team members** Nathan Chow, Jay Lin, Kourosh Mahvash, Kathleen Robertson, Craig Simms / **Structural Engineer** Fast + Epp Structural Engineers / **Mechanical Engineer** Integral Group / **Electrical Engineer** MMM Group / **Civil Engineer** AECOM / **Landscape Architect** Space2Place Design Inc. / **Contractor** Ledcor

Duchess Park Secondary

Client School District No. 57 (Prince George) / **Architect of Record** Hughes Condon Marler Architects / **Partner in Charge** Karen Marler / **Other design team members** / Laura Arpiainen, Kevin Bismanis, Tom Hudson, Craig Lane, Kourosh Mahvash, Ian McLean, Kurt McLaren, Kathleen Robertson, Dwayne Smyth, Jack Woo / **Structural Engineer** Bush, Bohlman & Partners / **Mechanical Engineer** Poole & Associates Mechanical Engineers Ltd. / **Electrical Engineer** Cobalt Engineering LLP (now Integral Group) / **Civil Engineer** L+M Engineering Ltd. / **Landscape Architect** Jay Lazzarin Landscape Architect / **Code** LMDG Building Code Consultants Ltd. / **Geotechnical Engineer** GeoNorth Engineering Ltd. / **Building Envelope** Spratt Emanuel Engineering Ltd. / **Energy Modeling** EnerSys Analytics Inc. / **Contractor** Western Industrial Contractors Ltd.

Steveston Firehall

Client City of Richmond / **Architect of Record** Hughes Condon Marler Architects / **Partner in Charge** Darryl Condon / **Other design team members** Jay Lin, Dwayne Smyth / **Structural Engineer** Fast + Epp Structural Engineers / **Mechanical Engineers** AME Consulting Group Ltd. / **Electrical Engineer** Roy Campbell Inc. / **Contractor** Stuart Olson Dominion Group

Building Blocks Playhouse

Client Canadian Forest Products Ltd. / **Architect of Record** Hughes Condon Marler Architects / **Partner in Charge** Darryl Condon / **Other design team members** Paul Fast, Federica Piccone / **Structural Engineer** Fast + Epp Structural Engineers / **Contractor** Haebler Group

Jasper Place Library

Client Edmonton Public Library / **Architect of Record** Hughes Condon Marler Architects and Dub Architects Ltd. in joint venture / **Partners in charge** Darryl Condon (HCMA) and Gene Dub (Dub) / **Other Design Team members** Steve DiPasquale, Stuart Maddox, Kourosh Mahvash, Vincent Siu (HCMA), Ciran Bonar, Michael Dub (Dub) / **Structural Engineer** Fast + Epp Structural Engineers / **Mechanical Engineer** Williams Engineering Canada Inc. / **Electrical Engineer** Williams Engineering Canada Inc. / **Civil Engineers** ISL Engineering and Land Services Inc. / **Landscape architects** Carlyle + Associates / **Code** LMDG Building Code Consultants Ltd. / **Acoustic** Brown Strachan Associates / **Contractor** Stuart Olson Dominion Construction

Mill Woods Library

Client Edmonton Public Library / **Architect of Record** Hughes Condon Marler Architects and Dub Architects Ltd. in joint venture / **Partners in charge** Darryl Condon (HCMA) and Gene Dub (Dub) / **Other Design Team members** Steve DiPasquale, Stuart Maddox, Kourosh Mahvash, Vincent Siu (HCMA), Ciran Bonar, Michael Dub (Dub) / **Structural Engineer** Fast + Epp Structural Engineers / **Mechanical Engineer** Williams Engineering Canada Inc. / **Electrical Engineer** Williams Engineering Canada Inc. / **Civil Engineers** Vital Engineering / **Landscape architects** PFS / **Code LMDG** Building Code Consultants Ltd. / **Acoustic** Daniel Lyzun & Associates / **Contractor** Ellis Don

Firm Profile

HCMA Architecture + Design, formerly Hughes Condon Marler Architects, is a firm of over 50 staff members that has been recognized internationally and nationally for service and design excellence. The open studio environment in both our Vancouver and Victoria offices supports dialogue and problem solving, which are fundamental to our collaborative approach to design. HCMA has worked on a broad range of building types including recreation, education, civic, residential, commercial, cultural, and health-care. Recognized leaders in sustainable design, HCMA continually strives to develop architecture that integrates environmental, social, and economic considerations. Our work is both regionally and nationally focused with active projects across Canada. Our services includes site analysis and feasibility studies, public process and stakeholder workshops, architectural design, interior design, master planning and urban design, green building and LEED certification, project management, and construction contract administration. We believe in leveraging the power of design excellence in order to contribute to the broad goals that make up a strong, healthy, and socially diverse society.

HCMA Partners

Darryl Condon
Architect AIBC, AAA, SAA, OAA, FRAIC, LEED® AP

Darryl Condon, Managing Principal at HCMA, studied architecture at McGill University's School of Architecture. For much of his over-twenty years of practice his focus has been on community-oriented projects. He has unique expertise in civic, community, recreation, sport and especially aquatic facilities. He has led the design and construction of highly innovative public projects including the West Vancouver Community and Aquatic Centres, the Vancouver Olympic Centre, the Aquatic Centre at Hillcrest Park, Sungod Recreation Centre, Whistler Public Library, Walnut Grove Community Centre, Saint-Laurent Sports Complex and the Grandview Heights Aquatic Centre. Over the past several years, his work has been recognized with over forty national and international awards for design excellence. He has lectured on issues related to sport and recreation facility design for groups such as the Canadian Parks and Recreation Association, British Columbia Recreation and Parks Association and Parks and Recreation Ontario. In 2009 Darryl was inducted into the College of Fellows of the Royal Architectural Institute of Canada.

Karen Marler
Architect AIBC, SAA, OAA, FRAIC, LEED® AP

Karen studied architecture at the University of Manitoba and at the Technical University of Nova Scotia, and then subsequently joined HCMA's predecessor firm, Hughes Baldwin Architects. Karen joined the Partnership in 1998. Throughout her approximately thirty years of practice, Karen has been involved in a wide variety of project types. Several of her key projects include Rogers Elementary School, Expo 86 Monorail Stations, University Hill Elementary School, Arbutus Walk Residences, Duchess Park Secondary School, UBC Boulevard, UBC Ponderosa Commons, UBC Alumni Building and the highly innovative and award-winning UniverCity Child Care Centre at Simon Fraser University. Karen has developed specific expertise with both residential and educational facilities. She has served as a member of University of British Columbia's Urban Design Panel, as a Guest Thesis Critic for the UBC School of Architecture and as a young woman's mentor for the YWCA of Greater Vancouver. In 2010, Karen was inducted into the College of Fellows of the Royal Architectural Institute of Canada.

Founding Partner

Stuart Rothnie
Architect AIBC, SAA, OAA, MRAIC, LEED® AP, PMP

Stuart studied Architecture at the University of Manchester in England. He went on to become an Associate with Squire and Partners in London for more than ten years prior to moving to Canada in 1992. Since arriving in Vancouver, Stuart has developed a diverse range of architectural experience and has been responsible for projects in the healthcare, recreation, educational, residential and commercial sectors. Stuart joined HCMA in 2000 and became a Partner in 2006. He has played a key role on many projects, including Sungod Recreation Centre, Langley Civic Facility, Vancouver Olympic Centre and led the planning work for the new BC Children and Women's Hospital project. Stuart is a qualified Project Management Professional (PMP) and has developed expertise in the management of multiple stakeholder groups and complex consultant teams. Stuart is past-chair of the West Vancouver Design Advisory Committee, past-member of the West Vancouver Planning Advisory Committee, and Co-Chair of the District of North Vancouver's Public Art Advisory Committee.

Carl-Jan Rupp
Architect AIBC, SAA, OAA, MRAIC, LEED® AP, BDB

Carl-Jan (CJ) graduated from Stuttgart University, Germany, where he received a Masters degree in Architecture and Town Planning with specializations in sustainable design, technology and urban design. In Stuttgart, he gained experience on diverse institutional, residential and commercial projects. Upon his return to Canada, he joined HCMA in 2000 and since that time has established unique expertise in educational, recreation, community, aquatic and institutional design. He has had key roles on many projects including Sungod Recreation Centre, Abbotsford Recreation Centre, Port Moody Recreation Centre, Legends Centre, Gordon Head Recreation Centre Expansion, Camosun College Campus Plan, and the Arts Centre at Cedar Hill projects. He has played a key role in the growth and development of the firm, and since 2005 has been managing the HCMA Victoria office and has been instrumental in its growth and development. Carl-Jan became a Partner with HCMA in 2012. He has provided community service in a variety of capacities including serving on the City of Saanich Urban Design Panel.

Roger Hughes
Architect AIBC, AAA, SAA, OAA, FRAIC, LEED® AP

Roger is a former Principal at HCMA and the founding partner of HCMA's predecessor firm. He was educated at the University of British Columbia and went on to complete continuing studies at the Architectural Association in London. After practicing for several years in the UK, Roger returned to Vancouver and, in 1976, he formed Roger Hughes Architects. Since that time he has designed and been responsible for a wide array of innovative projects including post-secondary, residential, civic, public, recreation, commercial, and urban design projects. Several of his key projects include Eileen Dailly Leisure Pool and Fitness Centre, Rogers Elementary School, Renfrew Branch Library, Spring Creek Fire Hall, Killarney Pool, and Chimo Aquatic and Fitness Centre. Over the forty years of his practice Roger has been recognized with numerous national and international awards for his work including several Governor General's Awards from the Royal Architectural Institute of Canada. In 1995, Roger was inducted into the College of Fellows of the Royal Architectural Institute of Canada.

Staff
1995–2015

Partners
Darryl Condon
Karen Marler
Stuart Rothnie
Carl-Jan Rupp

Founding Partner
Roger Hughes

Associates
Adam Fawkes
Paul Fast
Annerieke van Hoek
Michael Henderson
Melissa Higgs
Craig Lane
Jay Lin
Daniel Philippot

Staff
Aiden Callison
Miguel Castillo
Elena Chernyshov
John Christensen
Lindsay Csabak
Steve DiPasquale
Lindy Do
Derek Harris
Peter Johanek
Darryl Johnson
Ali Kenyon
Jessika Kliewer
Amanda Leier
Mona Lemoine
Wendy Li
Jay Lin
Ian McLean
Stephanie McWilliams
Kirsten Meissner
Steven Meldrum
Rance Mok
Courtenay Moore
Ryan Nelson
Karen Nolan
Miguel Orellana
Tony Osborn
Federica Piccone
Layla Pirelahi
Alec Ring
Andrew Rozen
Zubin Shroff
Heather Spinney
Philip Stolton
Alan Tse
Nicole Tuele
Annerieke van Hoek
Craig West
Rachel Wilson
Rob Wilson
Elise Woestyn
Dara Wone
Derek Wong
James Woodall
Nick Worth
Stephanie Zuke

Past staff
Chris Allen
Laura Arpiainen
Bonnie Barwick
Madelaine Beck
Karen Bier
Hugh Bitz
Marc Boutin
David Burdeny
Nancy Burton
Alan Bushby
Bruce Carscadden
Gaston Castano
Robert Cesnik
Ryan Cheng
Karla Christopher
Ben Cotter
Sarah Critelli-Kerr
Meike Czypulowski
Robert Drew
Nitra Famili
Wanda Felt
Michelle Fenton
Ward Fisher
Stephanie Forsythe
Marc Gaudreau
Shane Gee
Judith Glenn
Anna Grant
Carrie Gratland
Kent Grier
Andy Guiry
Jason Ha
Michelle Hayden
Phyllis Ho
Thomas Hudson
Bruce Jackson
Mona Jahedi
Peter Johanek
Peter Johannknecht
John Johansen
Elaine Jong
Miika Karpyshin
Gregory Knight
Sonya Kohut
Michel Labrie
Irwin Larman
Jin Lee
Mark Lee
Svend Lee
Don Lefaive
Andrew Li
Michael Lieu
Martin Liew
Natalka Lubiw
Kathy Lum
Florence Luong
Stuart Maddocks
Agatha Malcyzk
Leeanne Marshall
Jason Martin
Penny Martyn
Peter Mather
Ian Ross McDonald
Steve McFarlane
Kurt McLaren
Troy McNamara
Akbar Merchant
Kayna Merchant
Scott Mitchell
Julia Mogensen
Kirsten Mueller
Laura Murdoch-Fast
Katrin Myland
Heidi Nesbitt
Joseph O'Mahony
Patrick O'Sullivan
Steve Palmier
Jolene Parker
Ryan Pendleton
Jeff Pidsadny
Simon Pirquet
Scott Posno
Dejana Radjenovic
Margot Ready
Kathleen Roberts
Melissa Sanderson
Carey Ann Schaefer
Craig Sims
Jennifer Simpson
Alexander Smith
Dwayne Smyth
Brenda Solon
Jeanna South
Nicolas Sully
Ly Tang
Andrew Tankard
Joseph Thurrott
Celine Trinidad
Kelly Tupper
Bill Uhrich
Michel Veilleux
Tony Wai
Brian Wakelin
Ian Walsh
Nathan Webster
Patrick Wheeler
Tara Whelan
Bruce Whitty
Beatrice Wilhelm
Eli Wolpin
Jack Wu

We are thankful to our clients, our many staff members, consultants, and contractors who have been instrumental in the success of these projects. We have compiled these project credits from our available records, and apologize to anyone who may have been inadvertently omitted from this list.

Selected Projects

Current

Coronation Community Recreation Centre
Edmonton, MB

Coronation Park is an established and well-developed 35-hectare park. The new, multi-purpose Coronation Community Recreation Centre will integrate a wide variety of recreation interests and skill levels, respond to the needs of all ages and abilities, and will contribute to a sense of community by acting as a "community hub". The facility will complement and be physically connected to Peter Hemingway Fitness and Leisure Centre, an architecturally award winning aquatic and fitness centre. It will include a new fitness centre, gymnasia courts, a walking/jogging track, a International Cycling Union (UCI) sanctioned cycling track, and community spaces. Because of the significant change to the use of the park, the project includes an update of the Coronation District Activity Park Site Development Plan, including site access, parking, and location of any service areas and functions that are displaced through the Coronation Community Recreation Centre development. This is a joint venture project between HCMA and DUB Architects, in collaboration with FaulknerBrowns Architects.

Client City of Edmonton
Certification Targeting LEED® Silver

UBC Ponderosa Commons
Vancouver, BC

Ponderosa Commons serves a critical place-making role on campus. It marks the terminus of University Boulevard's spine and serves as a secondary gateway when approaching the campus from Marine Drive. Ponderosa Commons brings together Institutional Space, Community Space, Student Residences, and Landscape into a cohesive and vibrant mixed-use development. It is located at the intersection of University Boulevard and West Mall. The development comprises three key sites: Phase 1 East, Phase 1 West, and Phase 2 North. Ponderosa Commons is the first of 5 planned hubs on Campus. Hubs are mixed-use developments located in five areas of campus. These concentrations of development accommodate significant student housing, plus academic support services open to all students, faculty, and staff. Whether living in residence on campus or off campus, Hubs will function as neighbourhood living rooms for students, faculty, and staff attending the surrounding academic facilities. This project is in a joint venture with Kuwabara Payne McKenna Blumberg Architects.

Client University of British Columbia
Certification Targeting LEED® Silver

UBC Alumni Building
Vancouver, BC

The development of the University Boulevard Neighbourhood is intended to create a gateway to the campus as well as its heart and to reflect the University's ambition toward excellence. The UBC Alumni Centre will provide street level vitality and energy while establishing a strong aesthetic identity for the University and its alumni. UBC Alumni Centre, a 3700 m² facility containing a welcome centre, learning facilities, meeting spaces, offices and a café, is slated for occupancy at the beginning of 2014. The centre will be welcoming and accessible for alumni and students, its timeless design will express the collective values and legacy of the institution and its alumni. This project is a joint venture with Kuwabara Payne McKenna Blumberg Architects.

Client UBC Alumni Association
Certification Targeting LEED® Gold

Oak Bay High School
Oak Bay, BC

The new, 1,300 student school will replace two existing school buildings on the site. Designed to address 21st century learning principles, the design focuses on creating flexible learning environments, informal collaborative spaces, visual connections between spaces, and generous natural light and ventilation. The building is also designed to incorporate the changing technology and techniques used in teaching in the near and distant future with building systems providing for future flexibility. The school will include a state-of-the-art performing arts facility and a neighbourhood learning centre to host teens' programs, daycare, and other community programs. It will open September 2015, with the demolition of existing buildings and fields to be completed by September 2016.

Client School District No. 61
Certification Targeting LEED® Silver

Royal Bay Secondary School
Colwood, BC

The vision for the new Royal Bay Secondary school is a vibrant, modern, high-tech educational centre of excellence and a gathering place where students want to be. The new school will support 800 students from grades 9 to 12, with flexibility to support future expansion to 1200, and will include a Neighbourhood Learning Centre, a 350 seat theatre, as well as a rubberized, international standard athletic track. Located in a planned new community of 800 homes within the City of Colwood, the school will be the first building to be completed in this new neighbourhood, and is expected to be an anchor point for the future development. The school's roof is highly visible from the escarpment above, from the water by cruise ship, and from the air by plane. Rooftop play areas, courts, outdoor science project space and a student lounge area animate the rooftop in the daytime; at night, the clerestories transform the building into a glowing lantern that can be seen from the water and from above as a beacon, signifying the new community hub.

Client School District No. 62
Certification Targeting LEED® Gold

CESM Soccer Complex
Montreal, QB

The Saint Michel Soccer Complex is situated alongside a historic quarry in the City of Montreal. This site has been the centre of several important historic transformations, first as a quarry, then as a municipal landfill; now it is being transformed into a major municipal park and environmental demonstration project. The Soccer Complex is symbolized by its iconic long span roof structure, which appears to float above the complex. This project includes a full-size indoor soccer field, team locker rooms, and physiotherapy and training areas, spectator seating, food service, administration and multipurpose areas. This project is being completed in joint venture with Montreal-based Saucier + Perrotte architects.

Client City of Montreal
Certification Targeting LEED® Gold

St. Laurent Sports Complex
Montreal, QB

The winning entry in a design competition, The Saint-Laurent Sports Complex is a hub of sport and physical activity and a multipurpose gathering place that is green and alive. This 14,500 m^2 facility will be located on an important municipal axis. It will include an indoor soccer field, a 25-metre pool, a leisure pool, a sports gymnasium, a gymnastics gymnasium, a fitness room as well as several other multipurpose spaces. This project is being completed in joint venture with Montreal-based Saucier + Perrotte architects.

Client City of Saint-Laurent
Certification Targeting LEED® Gold

Anvil Centre
New-Westminster, BC

The City of New Westminster chose to locate its new Multi-Use Civic Facility (MUCF) in the centre of its downtown core to re-enforce the historic district. This signature gateway facility punctuates Columbia Street and reaffirms the City's commitment to invest in a vibrant mix of cultural programming for its citizens. The MUCF will include a studio theatre, banquet space, convention centre space, meeting space, a museum and archives, arts facilities, an art gallery, community recreation facilities, and a visitor's centre. In addition, there are three levels of underground parking below and six floors of office space above the MUCF. This project is being completed in association with Vancouver-based MCM Partnership Architects.

Client City of New Westminster
Certification Targeting LEED® Gold Certification

2012

Grandview Heights Aquatic Centre
Surrey, BC

Situated in Surrey, BC – one of Canada's most rapidly growing cities – the new Aquatic Centre is located in the center of the developing community of Grandview Heights. While still relatively undeveloped, the area is slated for major growth in the next 10 years, and the Centre is considered the first step in a larger vision for a campus of wellness, learning, healthy living, and sports excellence for the area. The aquatic and fitness programs are contained within an undulating roof form created by 5x10 glulam beams hung like cables from post-tensioned concrete buttress at each end of the building. The curving form of the roof rises were required to provide clearances for the Olympic dive platform on one end and a waterslide on the other. The waterslide is highly visible through the extensive glazing on the sites most prominent corner – inviting people to come in and splash. While the facility will be a draw for competitive swimmers and divers, and will serve as a key venue for regional, national and international competitions, it will also act as an important community hub.

Client City of Surrey
Certification Targeting LEED® Certification

UBC Faculty of Pharmaceutical Sciences
Vancouver, BC

Located at an important University entry point, the new facility for the Faculty of Pharmaceutical Science and Centre for Drug Research and Development functions as an active gateway into the academic core while reflecting the world-class quality of the faculty's research. Based on the pixelization of the canopy of two trees, the design concept demonstrates how the organic form of foliage can be transformed into a more Cartesian geometry. The 'trunks' house the auditorium volumes and reach to the sky as light wells. This project was completed in joint venture with Montreal-based Saucier + Perrotte architects.

Client UBC Properties Trust
Certification Targeting LEED® Gold
Awards Canadian Architect Award of Excellence • RAIC Governor General's Medals in Architecture 2014 • Architizer A+ Awards 2013 / Lieutenant Governor of BC Awards for Architecture 2013 • l'Ordre des Architectes du Québec 2013 • Ontario Association of Architects Awards - Design Excellence 2013 / Canadian Architect Award of Excellence 2011

2011

Fire Hall No. 15
Vancouver, BC

The existing wood fire hall was constructed in 1912. The challenge was to assess the potential heritage value of the existing structure and weigh this against its functional and operational short comings. Careful functional program, site, and facility analyses were conducted and several plans were considered. The chosen option will accommodate three apparatus bays, three bedrooms, an eight bed dormitory, kitchen, training and fitness facilities, fire prevention offices, general offices, hose drying tower, and generator backup. The project is to be designed as a post-disaster facility and is targeting LEED® Gold Certification.

Client Vancouver Fire & Rescue
Certification Targeting LEED® Gold

Vancouver Olympic / Paralympic Centre / Hillcrest Centre
Vancouver, BC

As the largest facility of its kind in the Vancouver Park Board system, the Hillcrest Centre stands as a bridge between an increasingly privatized world and the city as a living community. It is a demonstration of the aspirations of the community: to provide open and engaging recreation facilities; to revitalize an important public site; and to demonstrate environmental stewardship. Above all, the new facility demonstrates an energetic example of civic design. The impetus for this rejuvenation was the siting of the 2010 Vancouver Olympic Curling Venue, converted post-games to what is now the Hillcrest Centre. The Centre features a 52-meter pool as well as indoor and outdoor leisure water amenities, a large fitness centre, aerobic studios, multi-purpose rooms, a full-size gym, NHL-size ice rink, games room, childcare, curling club, and a branch library.

Client Vancouver Parks Board / Vancouver Organizing Committee (VANOC)
Certification Targeting LEED® Gold
Awards IAKS / International Olympic Committee Award for Exemplary Sports and Leisure Facilities 2013 • Athletic Business Facility of Merit Award 2012

2010

Robson Square Ice Rink
Vancouver, BC

Robson Square, designed in the 1970s by Arthur Erickson, is an icon of Canadian Architecture. This rehabilitation of the existing ice rink included membrane remediation, replacement of the existing concrete paving system, design and installation of a new expanded ice-rink surface, new lighting, and two large glazed stainless-steel domes, which provide shelter for the rink. This project was completed by HCMA as Architect of Record with Clive Grout Architect providing schematic design and design advocate architect services.

Client Province of British Columbia
Awards 2010 Canadian Steel Institute Award

2009

West Vancouver Community Centre
West Vancouver, BC

The West Vancouver Community Centre is an ambitious project that fulfills a number of objectives established by the community. The project unifies a dispersed grouping of existing community facilities and provides a "front door" to the Civic Centre site. The result is a series of highly dynamic spaces incased in a bold and simple form. With a gross building area of 7,710 m^2, the facility provides a comprehensive mix of community recreation and community health functions in a unique "Wellness" Centre that includes spaces for sport, dance, art, health education, health clinics, music, childcare, and a variety of social interaction.

Client District of West Vancouver
Certification LEED® Gold Certified
Awards IAKS / International Paralympic Committee Distinction for Accessibility 2013 • Chicago Athenaeum / European Centre for Architecture - International Architecture Award 2011 • Athletic Business Facility of Merit Award 2010 • Lieutenant Governor of BC Awards for Architecture 2010 • Real Estate Board of Greater Vancouver Commercial Building Awards 2010 • SAB Canadian Green Building Award 2010 • World Architecture Festival, Shortlist 2010

Gordon Head Recreation Centre
Saanich, BC

This project involved the expansion and renovation of the aging Gordon Head Recreation Centre in Saanich, BC. A series of internal renovations and rehabilitations were combined with a vibrant new addition of multipurpose rooms. The result is a significant transformation of the entire facility that will serve the current and future needs of the community.

Client District of Saanich
Certification Targeting LEED® Gold Certification

The Reach
Abbotsford, BC

The intention for this project was a memorable landmark building that would create a cultural nexus for the City of Abbotsford, attracting visitors, dynamic exhibitions, and interactive events to the community. The nearly 2,000 m^2 were conceived as three elements: a landmark entry tower, a great hall, and the back-of-house administration area. The facility offers flexible exhibition and event space, functional curatorial resources, and state-of-the-art environmental controls. This project was completed in association with Vancouver-based TRB Architecture.

Client City of Abbotsford

2008

2006

Abbotsford Recreation Centre
Abbotsford, BC

Chimo Aquatic and Fitness Centre
Coquitlam, BC

Port Moody Recreation Centre
Port Moody, BC

Legends Centre
Oshawa, ON

The third and final phase of a recreation multiplex, this addition includes a double gymnasium, multipurpose rooms, a youth centre, a fitness area, a running track, a seniors centre, a daycare, a café and change rooms. To preserves site area, new parking is located under the building expansion and is opened to adjacent site areas due to the contour of the site, which slopes to the south away from the existing facilities. A central spine runs north to south connecting the existing lobby and entry on the north to the new facilities terminating to the south.

Client City of Abbotsford

This aquatic facility provides a light-filled natatorium complete with a 25-metre lap pool, warm water leisure pool, water features, hot pool, steam and sauna. With an emphasis upon health and wellness the facility also includes a state-of-the-art weight training and cardio fitness facility. The facility is uniquely accessible for families and patrons with special needs and features a universal change room design. With a reduced front set-back, the facility entrance and plaza offers a dynamic "streetscape" feel.

Client City of Coquitlam
Awards Athletic Business Facility of Merit Award 2009 • Lieutenant Governor of BC Awards for Architecture 2009

This renovation and expansion project provides a major athletic and sport destination to the city and surrounding area. The new additions tie together three existing components—ice arena, curling rink, and social recreation centre—with new components including a second ice arena, a double gymnasium, running track, multipurpose spaces, tennis courts, all-weather artificial turf playing field, field house, a fitness facility complete with aerobics room, and change rooms with associated spa. The result is a unified comprehensive facility that addresses the current and future needs of the community.

Client City of Port Moody

As one of the fastest growing cities in Southern Ontario, Oshawa was seeking to develop an all-encompassing recreation and civic centre for its emerging population. The design team collaborated closely with the facility's operators to synthesize the unique needs of the ice arenas, aquatic and fitness facilities, seniors' centre, and library. To bring together the programming and siting objectives of this challenging project, the facility is designed along a central spine: an interior streetscape with views within and between activity spaces. Multiple entry points offer convenience to its users while giving the facility a fluid and open feeling. By resisting a formal front entrance, the building opens up on all sides, affording views to a creek and greenery to the east, basketball court to the north, and soccer fields to the south. This project was completed in joint-venture with local architectural firm, Barry Bryan Associates.

Client City of Oshawa
Awards Athletic Business Facility of Merit Award 2007 • Canadian Institute of Steel Design Award 2006

2005

2004

Killarney Community Pool
Vancouver, BC

When HCMA undertook the design of a replacement facility for the existing pool, the goal was to create a dynamic building for the community. The new facility provides a 25-metre lap pool, leisure pool, hot pool, multi-purpose space and related administration and changing facilities. The design transforms the character of the complex, opening it up to the sweeping views of the park and Coast Mountains to the north. This project also pioneers an innovative universal change room design in which locker spaces are open to view and patrons change in private cubicles. By eliminating the need for full height partitions and enclosing walls, the universal change room creates the opportunity to light the space naturally and improves safety and security.

Client Vancouver Board of Parks & Recreation
Awards IAKS / International Paralympic Committee Distinction for Accessibility 2011 • Lieutenant Governor of BC Awards for Architecture 2007 • Athletic Business Facility of Merit Award 2007

HCMA Vancouver Offices
Vancouver, BC

In-line with our philosophy of creating spaces that promote community and delight users, HCMA renovated our own Vancouver office under the LEED® Commercial Interiors Pilot Project. Small yet significant changes were made, including increasing the amount of natural light and the number of operable windows, as well as adding areas for socializing on outside decks surrounded by organic planters and fruit trees. The project received the first LEED®CI Certification in Canada.

Client HCMA
Certification LEED®CI Silver Certified

Township of Langley Civic Facility
Langley, BC

After several attempts to obtain funding, the Township of Langley abandoned plans to build an entirely new civic facility and instead decided to purchase and renovate an existing four-storey office building. The result is a facility that has unified staff, provides a civic presence in Langley, and acts as the flagship for the Township's municipal activities. In addition to municipal hall functions, the project provides a presentation theatre / council chamber, a branch library, a community Police Office, and a community recreation facility.

Client Township of Langley
Certification LEED®CI Silver Certified

Spring Creek Fire Hall
Whistler, BC

The design of this three-bay fire hall reflects a desire for protecting and minimizing impact to its natural setting in Whistler, BC. The project incorporates a variety of green building strategies including recycled materials, a green roof, local, low-toxicity building materials, natural ventilation, storm-water return, and end-of-trip amenities for cycle commuters. This LEED® Silver Certified fire hall serves an important civic function as a teaching facility for both "green building" principles and fire and safety training.

Client Resort Municipality of Whistler
Certification LEED® Silver-Certified

2003

2002

Azura Twin Towers
Vancouver, BC

Concord Pacific's Azura Towers offer residents uninterrupted water views of False Creek while successfully extending public access to this beach front precinct. The project consists of two 33-storey towers with a crescent of townhouses forming the edge to George Wainborn Park adjacent to the north shore of False Creek. Azura includes floor-to-ceiling glass, multipurpose space, and unique club-like fitness/leisure facilities. The design establishes two distinct but connected forms: a curved transparent window wall, anchored by a concrete rectangular block with recessed punched windows. The simplicity of these two shapes gives the towers their strength and establishes them as a gateway to the neighbourhood.

Client Concord Pacific Ltd.

West Vancouver Aquatic Center
West Vancouver, BC

The West Vancouver Aquatic Centre was a pioneer for new architectural ideas in aquatic and community facility design. Its spacious natatorium, abundant natural light, and dynamic engagement with public art all lend to a unique and dynamic user experience. A creative use of local wood, solar shading technology and a custom glulam glazing system further adds to its innovation. Extremely well-received by the community, this renewed facility is a dramatic demonstration of how architecture can reinvigorate a city's interest in health, wellness, and fitness. The project stands as an important civic gesture—helping to reinforce West Vancouver as a living and vibrant community.

Client District of West Vancouver
Awards IAKS / International Olympic Committee Award for Exemplary Sports and Leisure Facilities 2007 • IAKS International Paralympic Committee Distinction for Accessibility 2007 • Lieutenant Governor of BC Awards for Architecture 2005 • Athletic Business Facility of Merit Award 2005 • BCRPA Facility Excellence Award 2004

Fire Hall No 13
Vancouver, BC

This masonry fire hall achieves an appropriate civic presence while being respectful to the residential context of its setting. A combination of poured concrete, masonry, steel beams and wood come together as two truck bays, offices and living quarters for eight fire fighters. The sloped roof is punctuated by a series of recessed dormer windows at the lower level and projecting clerestory dormer windows above, promoting cross ventilation and reducing energy consumption. This project was completed in association with David Nairne and Associates.

Client City of Vancouver

Sungod Recreation Centre
Delta, BC

Sungod Recreation Centre revitalizes two previously aging buildings to form a dynamic new community facility. The rehabilitation and expansion of the arena and pool dispels any doubts about how architecture can retain existing structures and re-use existing buildings to provide a delightful user experience and even rejuvenate a community's interest in recreation and sport. Since its completion, visits to the facility have increased significantly. The expansion and renovation of the existing multipurpose community recreation facility provides a new ice sheet slab and boards for an ice arena, three new pools, common areas, multipurpose space, an outdoor courtyard, community sports gymnasium, weight room, fitness area and aerobic studios.

Client The Corporation of Delta
Awards Athletic Business Facility of Merit Award 2004

1999

1996

1994

Walnut Grove Aquatic Centre
Langley, BC

Centennial Square
Victoria, BC

University Hill Elementary
Vancouver, BC

Renfrew Library
Vancouver, BC

The Township of Langley needed an extensive expansion and renovation to this existing community centre. The objective was to provide an inspiring, light-filled, and energy-efficient recreation facility. Natural lighting, natural ventilation, and breathtaking mountain views provide users with a refreshing and inspirational recreation experience at Walnut Grove Community Centre. A striking conical skylight, long acoustical reflective panels, and large expansive glazing energize the aquatic facility and sufficiently light the facility without artificial aid during daylight hours. Visitors to the fitness area and aerobics studio are offered views of the pool area and the outdoors. This expansion and renovation includes a 6,000 m² aquatic centre and 3,000 m² renovations to the existing community centre.

Client Township of Langley
Awards RAIC Award of Excellence Contract Documentation 2001 • Athletic Business Facility of Merit Award 2000 • BCRPA Facility Excellence Award 2000 • Canadian Institute of Steel Design Award 2000 • Lieutenant Governor of BC Awards for Architecture 2000

HCMA's winning design in a province-wide design competition provided for a revitalization of Victoria's town centre and a unique blending of history into a new community precinct. The redevelopment included a new public library, adaptive re-use of the historic city hall, mixed-use seniors' centre/residential building, art gallery, commercial/retail buildings and civic offices. The scheme transforms the outdoor public spaces and provides a new civic core for the City of Victoria.

Client City of Victoria
Awards 1996 Winner of the Centennial Square Design Competition

Located within the Endowment Lands of the University of British Columbia, the school brings together students from diverse backgrounds and cultures. Interactive workshops with students, parents, and staff established design options that resulted in an open, colourful, and bright facility organized into two distinct areas: the general instruction area and an area accessible to the community after school hours. The site layout carefully respects the natural setting while offering safer pedestrian access and secure play environments. This project was started by HCMA's predecessor firm Hughes Baldwin Architects.

Client Vancouver School Board

The library provides bold civic design and sensitive siting within a park context while emphasizing community-use and public accessibility. An iconic roof extension greets patrons, while keeping out direct and potentially damaging sunlight. The library offers facilities for all demographics—quiet, light-filled carrels, seating areas, a media centre, a children's section (with lower ceilings), and a common area for families. Careful siting improves pedestrian movement around the library as well as the existing adjacent park and community centre. This project was completed by HCMA's predecessor firm Hughes Baldwin Architects.

Client City of Vancouver
Awards RAIC Governor Generals Award
AIA Western International Design

Awards

Listed awards include those won by HCMA Architecture + Design as well as its predecessor firms: Hughes Condon Marler Architects, Roger Hughes Architects, Hughes Baldwin Architects and Roger Hughes + Partner Architects.

RAIC Governor General's Awards for Architecture
UBC Faculty of Pharmaceutical Sciences / CDRD 2014
Renfrew Public Library 1997
Rogers Elementary 1992
Seascapes Condominiums - Medal 1990
Pacific Heights Housing Co-operative - Medal 1986
Sixth Estate Mixed-Use 1986

RAIC Award of Excellence Contract Documentation
Walnut Grove Community Centre 2001

RAIC National Urban Design Award
UBC University Boulevard 2006

Canadian Architect Award of Excellence
UBC Faculty of Pharmaceutical Sciences / CDRD 2011
Rogers Elementary School 1989

American Institute of Architects Urban Design Award
UBC University Boulevard 2006

AIA Western International Design Awards
Renfrew Branch Library 2000

Lieutenant Governor of BC Awards for Architecture
UBC Faculty of Pharmaceutical Sciences / CDRD - Merit 2013
West Vancouver Community Centre 2010
Whistler Public Library 2009
Chimo Aquatic and Fitness Facility 2009
Killarney Community Pool 2007
West Vancouver Aquatic Centre 2005
Walnut Grove Community Centre - Medal 2000
Eileen Dailly Leisure Pool and Fitness Centre 1995
Expo '86 Monorail Stations - Medal 1990

Edmonton Urban Design Awards
Jasper Place Branch Library - Merit 2013

Prairie Design Awards
Jasper Place Branch Library - Award of Merit 2014

Ontario Association of Architects Awards - Design Excellence
UBC Faculty of Pharmaceutical Sciences / CDRD 2013

Ordre des Architectes du Quebec - Grand Prix d'Excellence
UBC Faculty of Pharmaceutical Sciences / CDRD 2013

World Architecture Festival
Jasper Place Branch Library - Shortlist 2013
West Vancouver Community Centre - ONCE Foundation Award 2010
West Vancouver Community Centre - Shortlist 2010
Whistler Public Library - Shortlist 2009

Chicago Athenaeum / European Centre for Architecture - International Architecture Award
West Vancouver Community Centre 2011
Jasper Place Branch Library 2011

Architizer A+ Awards
UBC Faculty of Pharmaceutical Sciences / CDRD - 'Higher Education Institutions & Research Facilities' 2013

AZURE AZ Awards
UBC Faculty of Pharmaceutical Sciences / CDRD - 'Best Architecture Commercial & Institutional' 2013

Progressive Architecture Awards
St. Michel Soccer Complex - Citation 2014

Wallpaper* Design Awards
UBC Faculty of Pharmaceutical Sciences / CDRD - 'Best Lab' 2013

IAKS / International Olympic Committee Award for Exemplary Sports and Leisure Facilities
Hillcrest Centre - Bronze 2013
West Vancouver Aquatic Centre - Bronze 2007
Eileen Dailly Leisure Pool and Fitness Centre 2001

IAKS / International Paralympic Committee Distinction for Accessibility
West Vancouver Community Centre 2013
Killarney Community Pool 2011
West Vancouver Aquatic Centre 2007

Athletic Business Facility of Merit Award
Hillcrest Centre 2012
Aquatic Centre at Hillcrest Park 2011
West Vancouver Community Centre 2010
Chimo Aquatic & Fitness Facility 2009
Legends Centre 2007
Killarney Community Pool 2007
West Vancouver Aquatic Centre 2005
Sungod Recreation Centre 2004
Walnut Grove Community Centre 2000

BCRPA Facility Excellence Award
West Vancouver Aquatic Centre 2004
Walnut Grove Community Centre 2000

Canadian Design-Build Institute Award
Duchess Park Secondary School 2011

Canadian Housing Design Council Governor General's Award
Helen's Court Housing Co-operative 1985
1318 Thurlow Street Apartments 1985
Sixth Estate 1983
Matheson Heights Housing Co-operative 1983

AIBC Design Award
Sixth Estate 1983
Oakview Terrace Townhouses 1983
Begbie Square Courthouse Plaza 1981
Fairview Townhouses 1979

Interior Design Institute of BC Award
Architectural Institute of British Columbia Offices 1998

Urban Development Institute Award
River District Centre - Best 'Outside the Box' 2012
UniverCity Childcare Centre - Best Sustainable 2012
Tugboat Landing Phase 1 1994
River Terrace Townhouses 1987

Real Estate Board of Greater Vancouver Commercial Building Awards
Hillcrest Centre - Community Recreation Award of Excellence 2012
Hillcrest Centre - Overall Judge's Choice 2012
West Vancouver Community Centre 2010

The Nationals
River District Experience Centre - 'Best Presentation Centre' 2013

City of Vancouver Heritage Award
Architectural Institute of BC Office Renovation 1999
Pacific Heights Housing Co-operative 1986

Richmond Urban Design Awards
Steveston Fire Hall - Public & Institutional Buildings 2013

City of Burnaby Environment Award
Univercity Childcare Centre - Planning and Development 2012

New Westminster Royal City Builder Awards
Queen's Park Sub Acute Rehabilitation Unit 2006
700 Park – Glenview Veterans Rehousing 1998
Columbia Square Shopping Centre 1991
Columbia Towers 1991

Les Merites d'Architecture de la Ville de Quebec
University Laval TELUS Stadium - Public & Institutional Buildings 2013
University Laval TELUS Stadium - Special Jury Prize 2013

Globe Foundation / World Green Building Council Award
Vancouver Olympic / Paralympic Centre 2009

SAB Canadian Green Building Award
UNBC Bio-Energy Building 2014
UniverCity Childcare Centre 2013
West Vancouver Community Centre 2010
Whistler Public Library 2010

Wood First Champion Award
Vancouver Olympic/Paralympic Centre 2010

Good Wood Award
Vancouver Olympic/Paralympic Centre 2010

Wood Design Real Cedar Award
Whistler Public Library 2008

North America Wood Design & Building Awards
Aquatic Centre at Hillcrest Park 2012

Selected Publications

Canadian Wood WORKS! BC Wood Design Awards
UniverCity Childcare Centre - Honourable Mention 2014
Steveston Fire Hall 2012
Aquatic Centre at Hillcrest Park 2011
Butchart Gardens Carousel Pavilion 2011
Whistler Public Library - Architect Award 2009

Architectural Woodwork Manufacturers Association of Canada
UBC Faculty of Pharmaceutical Sciences / CDRD 2013

Canadian Institute of Steel Design Award
Robson Square Ice Rink Expansion and Plaza Revitalization 2009
Legends Centre 2006
Walnut Grove Community Centre 2000
Eileen Dailly Leisure Pool and Fitness Centre 1993

Masonry Institute of BC Design Awards
Hillcrest Centre 2012

The Canadian Home Builders' Association
The Ansonia at Arbutus Walk 1999

Consulting Engineering of BC Award of Excellence
UBC Faculty of Pharmaceutical Sciences / CDRD - Building Category 2013
Vancouver Olympic/Paralympic Centre 2010

Association of Consulting Engineering Companies
Jasper Place Branch Library 2014

Vancouver Regional Construction Association Silver Award of Excellence
UBC Faculty of Pharmaceutical Sciences / CDRD - Excellence in Sustainable Construction 2013

Canadian Society Landscape Architects Award of Excellence
UniverCity Childcare Centre 2013

CaGBC National Leadership Awards
UniverCity Childcare Centre 2013

EcoStar Award
St. Rose of Lima Catholic Church 2013

IES Illumination Award of Merit
UBC Faculty of Pharmaceutical Sciences / CDRD 2014

Berrisfor, Michael. *Generation Green: The Making of the UniverCity Childcare Centre.*
Canada: Ecotone Publishing, 2014.

Peters, Adele. "This coffee shop repels wireless signals so you won't be tempted by your phone".
FastCo. 18 July 2014. Online

Goncahr, Joann. "Teaching an Old Material New Tricks" *Architectural Record* July 2014. P 136–137

Bains, Meera. "What should gender–neutral washroom signs look like?"
CBC News March 28, 2014. Online.

Patton, Lindsey. "Nature + Nurture" *Green Building & Design* January/February 2014. Print

Woolliams, Jessica. "For the People".
Canadian Architect January 2014. P. 26–30

Boddy, Trevor. "Making Waves".
Canadian Architect Nov 2013. P 35–39

Southcott, Tanya. "Collaborative Cure".
Canadian Architect Sept 2013. P 18–23

Hume, Mark. " 'Cubist tree' blooms at new UBC sciences building."
The Globe and Mail May 29, 2013.

Rochon, Lisa. "Going with the grain, and building with wood."
The Globe and Mail March 29, 2013.

Weder, Adele. "Strong Medicine". *Azure* Mar/Apr. 2013. 55–57.

Livesey, Graham. "Big D Design in The Big E".
Canadian Architect Jan. 2013. P. 20–26

Bula, Frances."SFU Daycare Designed Backward, Starting with Green Materials".
Globe Advisor, 7 Aug. 2012.

McKnight, Zoe. "Builders, architects to create playhouses for housing charity".
Vancouver Sun, 28 June 2012.

Millar, Erin. "Only radical thinking will solve environmental problems".
The Globe and Mail, 30 May 2012.

"Jasper Place Library" Concept Magazine, Volume 139 2010: pp 124–27

Taggart, Jim. "Whistler Public Library". *Sustainable Architecture and Building Magazine.*
Issue Number 20, November/December 2010. P. 26–31

Taggart, Jim. "Vancouver Olympic / Paralympic Centre", Sustainable Architecture in Canada,
World Architecture Magazine, Issue 242, August 2010. P. 18–19, 66–71.

Kolleny, Jane F. "Whistler Public Library, British Columbia, Canada: Hughes Condon Marler Architects showcase locally sourced hemlock in Whistler's new public library". *Architectural Record* Oct. 2009. Print

Jen, Leslie. "Room to Read".
Canadian Architect Feb. 2009: 14–17. Print

Photography

Mark Boland
Pages 71 bottom, 74,

Darryl Condon
Pages 20–27, 130, 169–171

Dub Architects
Page 162

Alistair Heseltine
Page 116 right

Paul Joseph
Page 18

Hubert Kang
Cover, pages 6, 7, 54, 58, 60, 61, 64, 70, 71 top, 72, 73, 75, 126, 136, 137-151

Andre Kertesz
Pages 8, 9

Nic Lehoux
Pages 28, 33, 36, 37, 40, 41

Ryan Nelson
Pages 15 right, 76, 80, 81, 87, 90, 91, 92, 93

Gary Otte
Pages 12, 13, 14 top,

Martin Tessler
Pages 11, 14, 16, 19 bottom, 32, 34, 35, 39, 42–46, 50-53, 57, 59, 62, 63, 102, 108–110, 112, 113, 115, 116 left, 117-125

Book Credits

Darryl Condon

Darryl Condon, Managing Principal at HCMA, studied architecture at McGill University's School of Architecture. For much of his over-twenty years of practice his focus has been on community-focused projects, leading the design and construction of highly innovative public projects like the Whistler Public Library, West Vancouver Community Centre, the Jasper Place Branch Library and the Grandview Heights Aquatic Centre in Surrey, BC. Darryl's work has been recognized with over fifty national and international awards for design excellence. As well, he is currently the Vice President of the Architecture Institute of British Columbia and recently was appointed to the role of adjunct faculty at the University Of British Columbia, School Of Architecture and Landscape Architecture teaching a master's level course titled Social Sustainability in Practice.

Jim Taggart

Since leaving architectural practice in 1992, Jim has concentrated on public and professional education and communications in the areas of architecture, urban design, and sustainable development.

As a writer and editor, Jim's articles have appeared in professional, technical and general publications across North America, Europe and Asia. He is also the author or editor of more than a dozen books. His most recent work, *Toward a Culture of Wood Architecture*, received an international Independent Publishers (IPPY) award in 2012.

Jim has taught architecture at the British Columbia Institute of Technology since 2004, developing and delivering courses in history, theory, sustainability, and wood design. He is also the editor of the award-winning *Sustainable Architecture and Building Magazine* and advisor to its Canadian Green Building Awards program. Jim is a recipient of numerous awards including a Certificate of Recognition for services to the architectural profession in British Columbia, and an Innovation Award for the creation of its Architects in Schools program. He was inducted as a Fellow of the Royal Architectural Institute of Canada in 2010 and was the recipient of the Premier of British Columbia's Wood Champion Award in 2012.

Christopher Macdonald

Chris Macdonald is Professor in the School of Architecture and Landscape Architecture at the University of British Columbia. His professional education was at the University of Manitoba and the Architectural Association School of Architecture. He has been teaching design and related topics for 35 years and, prior to his tenure at UBC, taught at the AA School, the University of Texas and Sci-ARC. The work of his early practice —Macdonald and Salter— has been widely exhibited and published. Throughout his academic life he has contributed as author and curator to architectural discourse both local and dispersed, with particular emphasis on the imprint of locale upon emergent modern practice.

Melissa Higgs

Melissa Higgs trained as an architect at the University of Calgary Faculty of Environmental Design and became a registered architect in 2007 after returning to Vancouver. Melissa joined HCMA Architecture + Design in 2006 and has been an Associate since 2011. In the fall of 2013, Melissa was thrilled to have the opportunity to work with Darryl Condon to prepare and teach a course on a topic she is passionate about – Social Sustainability in Practice – at the University of British Columbia School of Architecture. As a practicing architect at HCMA, Melissa worked extensively on the West Vancouver Community Centre and is currently the Project Architect for the Grandview Heights Aquatic Centre in Surrey, BC. Melissa is an active mentor through the AIBC and currently sits on the AIBC Diverse Membership Working Group.

Alexandra Kenyon

Alexandra Kenyon is an AIBC Intern Architect at HCMA where she has played a significant role in the delivery of Royal Bay Secondary School on Vancouver Island and Minoru Complex in Richmond, BC, as well as in the development of their first book *POOLS: Aquatic Architecture*, and the creation of their iPad application. She is co-curator of Tangential Vancouverism, a research lab for new urban extensions of city life in Vancouver, which pilotted in 2012, and an architecture instructor at the Arts Umbrella in Vancouver.

Pablo Mandel

Pablo Mandel is a graphic design consultant specializing in architecture and art publications both printed and interactive. He has worked with some of the most renown architectural studios in the world. His book designs have won several awards, including the Canadian Society of Landscape Architects' National Merit Award 2011 for *Grounded*, and the Bookbuilders West's Certificate of Excellence. In addition to *PLACES*, he has collaborated with HCMA designing their first book *POOLS*, and the firm's iPad application. Pablo graduated from Buenos Aires University in 1995 with a degree in Graphic Design, and he is a Certified Member of the Society of Graphic Designers of Canada. His work can be seen at www.circularstudio.com.

PLACES

Acknowledgements

The development of this book continued the process of reinvestigation started by its companion book, POOLS: Aquatic Architecture. Through the process we have again enjoyed the opportunity to articulate the design philosophy that binds the work of each book. There have been many people involved in the production of this book and the projects that are contained within it.

Jim Taggart has played a key role which included providing his considerable writing skills as well as valuable research that supported the collective efforts. HCMA Associate Melissa Higgs provided an essay and editorial support. We are grateful to Christopher Macdonald for his introductory essay which frames the broader context for the book. A special thanks goes to Ali Kenyon who again played a vital role in the production of the book in terms of organization, editing, and critical thinking. Ali was instrumental to the success of this project.

My Partners, Karen Marler, Stuart Rothnie and Carl-Jan Rupp, as well as our former Partner, Roger Hughes, have all contributed in terms of leadership as well as through the projects that they were central to. We continue to be amazed by the caliber of our staff at HCMA and are grateful for the shared leadership provided by our Associates: Paul Fast, Adam Fawkes, Michael Henderson, Melissa Higgs, Craig Lane, Jay Lin, Daniel Philippot and Annerieke van Hoek. Our team shares a common dedication to excellence and we simply could not do what we do without them.

We continue to be fortunate to have exceptional clients, and the clients associated with the projects in this book are no different. Thank you for your trust, your challenges, and your support.

We remain committed to utilizing our skills to better the communities in which we live, volunteer, and work. Having the good fortune of working on public architecture comes with significant responsibilities. We embrace these responsibilities and look forward to additional opportunities to design the places where people and communities come together.

—Darryl Condon

HCMA

VANCOUVER
Suite 400
675 West Hastings
Vancouver BC
Canada V6B 1N2

T 604 732 6620
F 604 732 6695
E office@HCMA.ca

VICTORIA
Suite 300
569 Johnson Street
Victoria BC
Canada V8W 1M2

T 250 382 6650
F 250 382 6652
E office@HCMA.ca